The Mark Of A
WORLD CHANGER

Building Your Life With Character, Not Hype

RON LUCE

FOUNDER & PRESIDENT OF TEEN MANIA MINISTRIES™

OLIVER
NELSON

THOMAS NELSON PUBLISHERS
Nashville • Atlanta • London • Vancouver

*This book is dedicated
to the Teen Mania Interns
of 1995–96.
You guys embody what is written here.
You have proven that there are no limits
to the passion for God possible
in a human being.
Go make your mark on this world!*

Published in Nashville, Tennessee, by Thomas Nelson, Inc., Publishers, and distributed in Canada by Word Communications, Ltd., Richmond, British Columbia.

Unless otherwise noted, the Scripture quotations in this publication are taken from the HOLY BIBLE, NEW INTERNATIONAL VERSION. Copyright © 1973, 1978, 1984 by International Bible Society. Used by permission of Zondervan Publishing House. All rights reserved. Scripture quotations marked NKJV are from THE NEW KING JAMES VERSION. Copyright © 1979, 1980, 1982, Thomas Nelson, Inc., Publishers. Scripture quotations marked KJV are from the King James Version of the Holy Bible.

Library of Congress Cataloging-in-Publication Data

Luce, Ron.
    The mark of a WorldChanger : building your life with character, not hype / Ron Luce.
        p.   cm.
    Summary: A thirteen-week devotional designed to develop the character of a WorldChanger.
    ISBN 0-7852-7251-8
    1. Teenagers—Prayer-books and devotions—English. [1. Prayer books and devotions. 2. Conduct of life. 3. Christian life.] I. Title.
BV4850.L85 1996
248.8′3—dc20

96–9470
CIP
AC

Printed in the United States of America.

3 4 5 6 — 01 00 99 98 97

CONTENTS

WEEK 7

WEEK 8

WEEK 9

WEEK 10

WEEK 11

WEEK 12

WEEK 13

Acknowledgments

I would like to thank all the people who have contributed to this work in so many ways. My assistant, Brenda Tibbles, has been an incredible asset, as well as the young ladies who work with her: Tonia, Alicia, and Lora.

Thanks of course to my awesome wife of twelve years, Katie, who is my best friend.

I must also thank Joni Jones again for being such an integral part of this work.

Introduction

This book is designed to help you change the world. God is looking for a new kind of young person who is ready to stand up and be counted. He is looking for a young person who is ready to work for God's agenda for this world. This book, *The Mark of a WorldChanger,* is designed as a devotional. It provides something to do every day in your quiet time. It is written to help you implement change in your life. There are Scriptures for you to memorize and things for you to write. It is designed to help you be a different person by the time you complete it. There is actually something for you to work on every single day to help you become more like Jesus, more and more a person who will change this world.

God is not looking for people who will blend in. He is looking for people who are ready to make a difference. Thousands of young people already have signed up to make this kind of strategic difference in the world. As you read through this book and apply these principles to your life, you will be pushed out of your comfort zone and compelled to do something different with your life.

Go through it with a friend so you can pray together, challenge each other, and really apply what you are learning here.

By the time you are finished, you will be able to say with thousands of others that you truly have the mark of a World-

Changer on your life because you will have developed the character of a WorldChanger in the way you live.

This book is a thirteen-week devotional. Get psyched up now about going for it every day and doing everything the book asks you to do. Some days you will write down your thoughts or a Scripture. Other days you will memorize a Scripture verse or passage.

Don't just read this book—*do* this book. Do everything in it—and you will be marked. People will see you and think, "What is different about you?" They will see that you are marked with character. You are set apart. You are not some part-time, namby-pamby, mealymouthed, yellow-bellied, halfhearted, lukewarm, thumb-sucking baby Christian. People will see that you are a WorldChanger through and through!

I want to encourage you to grab a friend to go through this book together. Commit to do it every day in your quiet times and then check up on each other. Hold each other accountable. Stay in each other's face. Be like Paul and Silas, and change the world together.

I COMMIT

TO GO ALL THE WAY THROUGH

THIS DEVOTIONAL.

I WILL START

ON _____

AND PLAN TO FINISH

ON _____.

_____
WORLDCHANGER'S SIGNATURE

_____
ACCOUNTABILITY PARTNER'S SIGNATURE

_____
YOUTH PASTOR'S OR PARENT'S SIGNATURE

WEEK 1

What Is a WorldChanger?

A Different Kind of Christian

A WorldChanger is someone who is committed to do just that, change the world. A WorldChanger is not someone who blends in. A WorldChanger sticks out. A WorldChanger stands up ready to make a difference. A WorldChanger goes beyond the usual expectations of Christianity. A WorldChanger finds the most intense demands that Jesus places on Christians and doesn't shy away from them but goes after them with all of his heart. A WorldChanger does whatever it takes to get the job done. A WorldChanger pursues God passionately. She is not just doing it because her parents make her or because the youth pastor bribes her. A WorldChanger has been radically, completely, and totally changed by the relationship with God.

Christianity is not some boring thing that WorldChangers halfheartedly commit to just because they've been in church their whole lives. They are not hanging on to their parents' Christianity. They have found Jesus for themselves. They have found that Jesus died for them—not just for Mom and Dad and not just for the pastor. And because Jesus died for them, they are ready to give their lives for Him. Christianity is not just lip service for WorldChangers. WorldChangers have a fervor to seek God with all of their hearts, and they are going to do everything they can to let the world know that God is real and that He is alive.

WorldChangers are not stuck in a bunch of boring rules and regulations, but they have the fire of the living God burning inside them. And they just can't keep it to themselves. World-Changers are serious about learning the Word of God and then taking that Word and applying it to their lives. WorldChangers are constantly changing and becoming more and more like Jesus. WorldChangers develop a vision for the world and do everything they can to take the living Christ to a lost and dying world.

WorldChangers are sick and tired of a watered-down, namby-pamby Christianity. They want the real thing and don't care how hard it hits them or what parts of their lives they have to change. They are sick and tired of the attitude that lukewarm Christians bring into the church, and they are ready to do something about it. They are especially ready to attack attitudes in their own lives.

MARK 12:29–30

"THE MOST IMPORTANT [COMMANDMENT]," ANSWERED JESUS, "IS THIS: 'HEAR O ISRAEL, THE LORD OUR GOD, THE LORD IS ONE. LOVE THE LORD YOUR GOD WITH ALL YOUR HEART AND WITH ALL YOUR SOUL AND WITH ALL YOUR MIND AND WITH ALL YOUR STRENGTH.'"

A WorldChanger loves the Lord with all of his heart, soul, mind, and strength and loves his neighbor as himself. Write this Scripture down. Carry it with you all day today. Begin to pray over what you've just learned about a WorldChanger. Ask yourself, Do I have what it takes to become a WorldChanger? I know you do because anybody who is willing has the potential to change the world.

What Is the Fire?

What does it really mean to be on fire? What do people mean when they tell you that you need to be on fire as a Christian? What are your youth pastor and parents really trying to get you to do when they say you need to live completely for God? Tell me what you think it means to be on fire for God.

We are told to do so many things as Christians that we don't know where to begin. We've heard so many sermons on things to do, we don't know what to do first. Then we feel really guilty or incompetent as Christians because we can't possibly keep up with the whole list of things we've been told we're supposed to do. What is the big picture? What are we supposed to do? What are we really supposed to be? What does a blazing, on-fire radical really look like? What would you call that kind of Christian? I call her a WorldChanger. A WorldChanger is not just somebody who screams JESUS really loud at concerts or goes to all of the Christian activities, retreats, conferences, and camps or wears Christian T-shirts. A WorldChanger LIVES differently. She has something beating in her heart.

And that's how I have developed the WorldChangers 2000 idea. It gives young people a mark to aim for. WorldChangers are marked and defined by ten specific challenges that they have committed to live out. These challenges are not something to get hyped up about during one week at a camp. They are not something to get emotional about and try to live for a month or two. These challenges are very specific things. And I'm convinced that if you live them—really commit to go for them—God will use you to rock your world while you're young.

I don't want to give you a list a thousand miles long of a million things you need to do in order to be a radical Christian. Just do these ten. Don't do any more, don't do any less, and I'm confident that you'll change the world. Take a look at these ten challenges right now:

1. **I Commit to Keep My Relationship with Jesus Alive by Keeping My Quiet Times.**
2. **I Commit My Mind to God.**
3. **I Commit to Systematically Study the Bible.**
4. **I Commit to an Accountability Friendship.**
5. **I Commit to a Lifestyle of Worship and Holy Actions.**
6. **I Commit to Holy Courtship Instead of Dating.**
7. **I Commit to Honor My Parents.**
8. **I Commit to My Church and My Youth Group.**
9. **I Commit to Start a Revolution.**
10. **I Commit to Go on a Mission Trip While I'm a Teen.**

As you read this list, make a commitment to be the kind of Christian who makes a difference in this world. If you are willing

MISSIONS IS...
an adventure for God.
—Anthony

to make this commitment right now, sign the World-Changers 2000 certificate at the back of this book (see page 225).

As you go through this text in your quiet time, you will learn different areas of character as a World-Changer. You need to develop them to live up to each one of these challenges. I encourage you today to commit to be one of the thousands who go for it. Don't just hang out with your Christian life, but aspire to change the world.

A Higher Standard

A WorldChanger is committed to a higher standard. Too much of teenage Christianity is plagued by people who are constantly living in compromise. They see their friends make commitments but do the opposite of what they promised. They see people go back and forth, up and down in their walk with God. But a WorldChanger wants to take the gospel seriously. Too many people act as if the commandments in the Scripture are just suggestions. They think Jesus really didn't mean for us to love our enemies or lay down our lives for each other. But a WorldChanger sees that when Jesus made a command, He absolutely meant it, and a WorldChanger is determined to live up to that standard.

WorldChangers go against the grain of compromise and lukewarm Christianity. WorldChangers want a higher standard of purity and holiness in their lives. They want clean hearts and clean minds so that God can speak in them and they can be used by the living God to change this world. WorldChangers see things that other people get away with, but they don't want to get away with that stuff. They know they could compromise and just melt down and be lukewarm Christians, but they know there is something more to the Christian life than just going through the motions and going to church. Too many young people are trying to get away with things with their parents all the time. They do the same thing in their Christianity, seeing what they can get away with before God and still make it to heaven.

Do you have areas of compromise in your life? What is one thing that you can do today to begin to turn that around?

A WorldChanger is different. A WorldChanger doesn't try to get away with stuff. He tries to keep his heart clean and pure, and if he crosses the line of sin, he humbles himself and repents as soon as he can because he wants to live a pure and holy life before God. A WorldChanger sees that she could get away with a lot of things, but she chooses to live up to a higher standard because she wants to be a more effective Christian. She wants to make a difference.

Today, I challenge you to commit to that higher standard. Commit to do what's right even though everyone else may not be doing it. Commit to living a more pure and more holy life even though it may not be the popular thing to do. It is only in living up to these commitments that God will trust you in changing other lives in this world. Now is your chance to join thousands of others who have jumped on board and said they, too, want to live at a higher standard of Christianity and make sure that their lives count for eternity.

Are You Hungry?

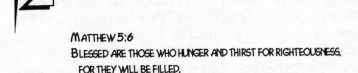

MATTHEW 5:6
BLESSED ARE THOSE WHO HUNGER AND THIRST FOR RIGHTEOUSNESS,
FOR THEY WILL BE FILLED.

W rite out Matthew 5:6 in your own words as you would explain it to someone your age.

WorldChangers are not just committed to a bunch of rules; they have a passion for God. They don't just want to know the Book; they want to know the God who wrote the Book. They want to know the Spirit and the heartbeat of the living God who inspired the Book. WorldChangers passionately pursue the living God. They can't stand the thought of going to church and just sitting there. They want an encounter with God. They can't stand the thought of just having quiet times. They want to meet with the living God. WorldChangers don't just go through the motions of a worship service. They bow before the throne of the holy God and have a face-to-face encounter with Him as they worship.

WorldChangers are hungry and thirsty for righteousness. They are hungry and thirsty to have a heart-to-heart encounter with God on a regular basis. They yearn for more of God's presence in their lives, and they will do anything to get it. They'll fast. They'll pray. They'll do everything they can to live holy and right. WorldChangers follow rules because they have a personal passion for God burning in their souls.

Already tens of thousands of young people have joined this quest for God. WorldChangers are no longer satisfied just going to youth group and then going home. It's not enough just to feel emotional about God on a retreat. It's a passion that burns in their hearts every single day. WorldChangers wake up crying, "God, I want more of You! God, I want to seek You today. I want to know You today." They feel an emptiness that can be filled only by the presence of the living God.

Memorize Matthew 5:6. Meditate on it. Chew on it all day long. Ask God to stir up a holy hunger and passion in your heart to know Him.

Not Just Talking About It

MATTHEW 28:19
GO THEREFORE AND MAKE DISCIPLES OF ALL THE NATIONS, BAPTIZING THEM IN THE NAME OF THE FATHER AND OF THE SON AND OF THE HOLY SPIRIT (NKJV).

WorldChangers are serious about making a difference. WorldChangers want to know God and to make Him known. They want their lives to count for eternity. They fervently go after doing something that affects other people's lives. WorldChangers have had an encounter with God that is so real they can't keep it to themselves. WorldChangers see a Scripture such as the Great Commission in Matthew 28:19 and know it wasn't just for the disciples. This command is for everybody.

WorldChangers can see that Jesus repeatedly encouraged His disciples to make a difference. He sent them out two by two. He sent them out in groups. He sent them out from village to village. He was constantly equipping them, training them, and preparing them to change the world. WorldChangers see that this is still Jesus' plan today, and they are actively involved in doing everything they can to make a difference. WorldChangers don't want to wait until they become adults to make a difference. They want to begin right now in school, in work, on a sports team, in the family, and in the church. WorldChangers want to make a difference.

WorldChangers don't just grunt through high school. They don't just grunt through youth group. They look for opportunities right now to make their mark and do something to show others the hand of God working in their lives. WorldChangers are serious about making an eternal impact. They are not haphazardly hoping that people will see Jesus in their eyes. They make serious plans. They use their energy right now to wake people up and show them that Jesus is alive.

What can you do to use your energy for God today?

Begin to ask the Lord,

Lord, what can I do today to make a difference? God, please plant deep down in my heart a passion to change the world. Give me the seriousness I need to make it not just a bunch of hot air and empty words but a productive life for Your kingdom. In Jesus' name, amen.

Giving Yourself Away

Luke 9:23
Then [Jesus] said to them all: "If anyone would come after me, he must deny himself and take up his cross daily and follow me."

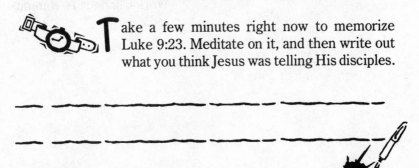

Take a few minutes right now to memorize Luke 9:23. Meditate on it, and then write out what you think Jesus was telling His disciples.

WorldChangers are committed. They are serious about keeping their word. They are serious about doing whatever it takes to live the gospel. We see too many people who say one thing and do another. Most of us don't have enough good examples of what commitment is all about.

Jesus said that when you come after Him, you must deny yourself and pick up your cross. Denying yourself and taking up your cross is preparing to die. A WorldChanger sees that strong commitment and doesn't scoff at it. Many people say they would die for Christ. But when it rains, they won't go to church because they don't want to get their hair messed up.

A WorldChanger says, "Whatever it takes for God, I'm going for it. Whatever Jesus wants of me, it already belongs to Him."

People are the same throughout the world —we all need God.
—Lauren

A WorldChanger takes the same commitment that he made when he gave his life to Christ, and he makes his commitment to change the world just as seriously because the world is desperately in need. A WorldChanger keeps her word when she gives it to the Lord or anyone else. A WorldChanger is committed.

It's a Lifestyle

I want to emphasize strongly that WorldChangers isn't a club or an organization that you join. A WorldChanger is who you are. As a WorldChanger, you have had your world changed so much by Jesus that you are passionately and radically committed to Him and to helping other people have the same kind of experience that you have had.

Based on what you have read this week, describe a World-Changer in your own words.

Now you can see what the big picture of WorldChangers 2000 is all about. It is time for you to join the ranks with tons of other

MISSIONS IS...
serving.
—Virginia

people who are ready to make a real difference. One by one WorldChangers are rising up and saying that they're sick and tired of Christian games and they're ready to make a difference. They are becoming part of God's elite army of special forces to take a whole generation back to God with His power.

I want to encourage you to sign on to the ten challenges and say, "Yes, in Jesus' name, I'm going for it!" Make a commitment right now to apply these character traits to your life so you can make your life count for eternity.

WEEK 2

The Mark of a WorldChanger

What Is the Mark of a WorldChanger?

2 PETER 1:5–9
FOR THIS VERY REASON, MAKE EVERY EFFORT TO ADD TO YOUR FAITH
GOODNESS; AND TO GOODNESS, KNOWLEDGE; AND TO KNOWLEDGE,
SELF-CONTROL; AND TO SELF-CONTROL, PERSEVERANCE; AND TO PERSEVERANCE,
GODLINESS; AND TO GODLINESS, BROTHERLY KINDNESS; AND TO BROTHERLY
KINDNESS, LOVE. FOR IF YOU POSSESS THESE QUALITIES IN INCREASING MEASURE,
THEY WILL KEEP YOU FROM BEING INEFFECTIVE AND UNPRODUCTIVE IN YOUR
KNOWLEDGE OF OUR LORD JESUS CHRIST. BUT IF ANYONE DOES NOT HAVE
THEM, HE IS NEARSIGHTED AND BLIND, AND HAS FORGOTTEN THAT HE HAS BEEN
CLEANSED FROM HIS PAST SINS.

 Take five minutes right now and memorize 2 Peter 1:5–9. These verses talk about developing character in your life, which is exactly what this book is about—developing character.

What is character?

You develop character one step at a time, one day at a time, one piece at a time—in other words, "in increasing measure." Many Christians are trying to do too many things *for* God, but they may do nothing at all in their walk *with* God. They don't add anything to their faith.

MISSIONS IS...
getting out of your comfort zone.
—Robin

They just keep going to church and youth group. Peter challenges us to add things to our faith that will help us build a life of godly character. It is great to have faith in the Lord, but the Bible is very clearly saying that you need to *add* things to your faith. You need to put some ingredients into your life showing that you do have faith.

When your faith is real, you can't stand just to be full of lip service. You have to have some substance in your life. That's what a WorldChanger does. You commit to the ten challenges, and you build substance into your life. When people look at you, they see a glimpse of what Jesus looks like.

What Is Character?

2 PETER 1:5-9
FOR THIS VERY REASON, MAKE EVERY EFFORT TO ADD TO YOUR FAITH
GOODNESS; AND TO GOODNESS, KNOWLEDGE; AND TO KNOWLEDGE,
SELF-CONTROL; AND TO SELF-CONTROL, PERSEVERANCE; AND TO PERSEVERANCE,
GODLINESS; AND TO GODLINESS, BROTHERLY KINDNESS; AND TO BROTHERLY
KINDNESS, LOVE. FOR IF YOU POSSESS THESE QUALITIES IN INCREASING MEASURE,
THEY WILL KEEP YOU FROM BEING INEFFECTIVE AND UNPRODUCTIVE IN YOUR
KNOWLEDGE OF OUR LORD JESUS CHRIST. BUT IF ANYONE DOES NOT HAVE
THEM, HE IS NEARSIGHTED AND BLIND, AND HAS FORGOTTEN THAT HE HAS BEEN
CLEANSED FROM HIS PAST SINS.

Meditate on this Scripture today. Write out how you think it would be said in a teen's words.

Webster's New Collegiate Dictionary defines *character* as "one of the attributes or features that make up and distinguish the individual; mental and ethical traits marking and individualizing a person; a person marked by notable traits; moral excellence and firmness." Character is a distinctive mark of what makes something or someone unique. God is looking to build character in us so that we have a distinct mark on our lives that we are Christians. Character is moral fiber. It is the difference between a loudmouthed hot-air Christian and somebody who really lives what he believes.

Character is a collection of godly habits and a godly lifestyle. A person of character will live in a righteous and holy way and do things the way God wants them done. Character makes your life stable and firm so it cannot be moved. It builds a reputation that people have confidence in you, and they know they can count on you to act or respond consistently because you have that kind of character built in you.

I know that God will use me if I am willing.
—Andy

Week **2**

DAY **3**

Why Is Character Important?

1 Timothy 4:12
DON'T LET ANYONE LOOK DOWN ON YOU BECAUSE YOU ARE YOUNG, BUT SET AN
EXAMPLE FOR THE BELIEVERS IN SPEECH, IN LIFE, IN LOVE, IN FAITH AND IN PURITY.

Many times others look down on young people in their
Christianity because they don't have character. They
just have lip service. They go back and forth, up and down,
depending on their emotions, depending on their mood swings.
Character separates us from the world. The world mocks us as
young Christians. It mocks Christianity in general because
Christians are full of lip service, but they hardly ever back it up
with their actions. It is time for that to stop. It is time for
somebody to stand up and say, "I'm going to do what I say I
believe, and I'm going to live it. I'm going to build into my life
godly habits that make me distinct from this world."

How would you like it if you never knew what your parents
were going to do when you asked them for basic things? You
could ask them for a glass of water, and they might bring you a
glass of water or a glass of poison. We need to show the world

what to expect from Christians. Throughout His whole life Jesus described God's character and His kingdom. When He talked about healings and told parables, He was describing what was typical in the kingdom of God.

Character has to do with being consistent regardless of the circumstances. People need to know that our relationship with Jesus is so real it has permanently changed our lives. We aren't just changed whenever we might feel in a good mood. Character is about living the gospel. Jesus said, "Let your light so shine before men, that they may see your good works and glorify your Father in heaven" (Matt. 5:16 NKJV). Having character is doing a lot more living and a lot less talking. Let your living do the talking. Somebody once said, "I need to preach every day and all day long and use my mouth only when necessary." In other words, you need to preach with your life, with your character, by the way you live.

What does it mean to you to "preach with your life"?

Character is important because through it, people will see a glimpse of what God is like. Most people have no idea what the living God is really like, and the only way they can find out is to look at Christians. If they don't see character in our lives, then they won't see what God is like. We are the body of Christ. We are the representation of God on this earth. We need to build godly habits into our lives so that when people look into our eyes and look at our lives, they'll see a glimpse of what the living God is like. We don't want to misrepresent the awesome holy God in any way. We have to build character into our lives. Continue to meditate on 2 Peter 1:5–9 all day today.

The Need for Character

Our society is in desperate need of character. Lack of character is often brought out by opposing candidates in election campaigns, and the public doesn't seem to think that the issue is very important. Many people don't seem to care if the candidates are cheating on their spouses. They don't seem to care if candidates are acting unethically. People seem more concerned about candidates' speaking abilities than about whether they have character in their lives. There is an incredible vacuum of character in the lives of many politicians, businesspeople, and even Christians.

When people hear of a preacher or minister, some wonder, "What is he doing to scam people out of their money?" or "What is he really in this for?" This is the very opposite of what Jesus intended. We Christians are supposed to be the standard the rest of the world looks to. People should see in us what is pure and holy. Unfortunately, many Christians have been tricked into believing that since it seems unimportant to the world to have strong character, it doesn't need to be important to us, either.

But the very opposite is true—God demands that we have character. He demands that we live like Him if we are going to represent Him.

Character is the development in your life of *qualities that look like God*. And in a world that doesn't value God or godly habits you may think that you are doing pretty good just by going to church. But you must develop these distinctive traits in your life the way that God would want them. God doesn't measure your maturity as a Christian by how much you go to church. *He measures it by obedience*. The more obedient you are, the more character you'll have in your life. It doesn't help God if you just go to church your whole life and get gray hair and die. He is looking for people who are determined to live His Word and be obedient. He is looking for people who will prove that they love Him by building His character into their lives. He is tired of people just going through the motions and speaking spiritual language but being bankrupt in character.

Today is the day to determine to go for it. In the midst of a world that doesn't seem to care about character, even in the body of Christ where some people don't seem to care about character in the church, we must be a young, fiery army determined not to let people mock us because we don't line up with the world.

Think of people whose lives you think you could learn from. Name the people in your life with character.

You must be determined to build a firm foundation so that when people look at you, they see a glimpse of what God looks like. You must build character into your life.

Personality Versus Character

Many people confuse personality with character. Some people can schmooze their way through life with a very funny personality. They can always make people laugh, and they are very popular. But some people who know how to make others feel good with a smile or with compliments learn to be manipulative to get their own way. Some people think that being popular, always having the funniest joke, or saying the most spiritual thing is having character. But all of these are substitutes for character. Some people are like chameleons. Just as chameleons change color to adapt to their environment, some people change personality.

What is your personality like?

Remember, personality is not character. Everybody has a personality, but not everybody has character.

Many people feel deficient because they don't have as funny, witty, or attractive a personality as another person does. They are not the life of the party. But God is not looking for people to be the life of the party; He is looking for people with character. He is not looking for people who can blend in or change colors wherever they go so others will like them; He is looking for people with character. He is not looking for people who can always have the funniest joke; He is looking for people with character. He wants people with godly habits built into their lives. He wants people who are the same whether they are in front of a lot of people or alone before God. He is looking for people with character.

Some people put a lot of energy into trying to develop personality so they will be more like another person. God cares much less about your personality traits than about your godly habits that show you are serious about what you believe. You can have an incredibly funny, witty, attractive personality but still be bankrupt in character.

Building character is not just about developing your personality. It is about making commitments and building godly habits into your life. No matter what mood you might be in, no matter who you might be around, there is something in you that is always in you, that is consistent, when you have character. The fact is, it's not people with witty personalities who succeed because many times personality will get them in trouble. It is people with solid character who succeed. They succeed in their walk with God, in their business affairs, and in life in general. And they succeed in changing the world because they have character and not just a flashy personality.

Begin to ask God right now to show you areas of character that you need to build into your life. Begin to pray for God to build character in you and not just for a personality like someone else's.

Gifting Versus Character

S ome people confuse gifting with character. They think if they are really talented in something, then they have character, so they want to be really good in sports, academics, or Scripture memorization. All these things are good, but they are not a substitute for character.

The problem can come when you become really good at something, and you become really popular and others begin to admire you. Unfortunately, when you get really good at something and people look up to you, you end up letting people down if you don't have moral character. That has happened over the years with Christian leaders and other heroes. Others looked up to them or rallied around them because of their giftings, but they didn't have the character to sustain them, so they fell. Look at sports heroes like Mike Tyson and Magic Johnson. Their giftings put them on a platform where everyone looked up to them, but then it was discovered that both of them were involved in very undignified things.

You need to develop your gifting—that's true—but you can't

develop your gifting instead of your character. If you have to make a choice, always choose character.

Character is a collection of godly habits. Meditate on 2 Peter 1:5–9 all day. It's not enough to be an airhead Christian and say you have faith. You have to add things to your faith that will build into you a lifestyle of godly habits and actions. Somebody might be good enough in sports to gain a reputation and even a little notoriety, but it is much more important to be good at loving God, being kind to others, keeping your word, and having other character traits of a WorldChanger.

How can your specific gifting work with your character to further the kingdom of God?

I want to encourage you to start building your character and not just your gifting because your character will make you a long-term success. Your gifting will add to it. Don't build your life on gifting; build it on character.

Having Character Propels You to a Different Level of Christianity

2 PETER 1:5–9

FOR THIS VERY REASON, MAKE EVERY EFFORT TO ADD TO YOUR FAITH GOODNESS; AND TO GOODNESS, KNOWLEDGE; AND TO KNOWLEDGE, SELF-CONTROL; AND TO SELF-CONTROL, PERSEVERANCE; AND TO PERSEVERANCE, GODLINESS; AND TO GODLINESS, BROTHERLY KINDNESS; AND TO BROTHERLY KINDNESS, LOVE. FOR IF YOU POSSESS THESE QUALITIES IN INCREASING MEASURE, THEY WILL KEEP YOU FROM BEING INEFFECTIVE AND UNPRODUCTIVE IN YOUR KNOWLEDGE OF OUR LORD JESUS CHRIST. BUT IF ANYONE DOES NOT HAVE THEM, HE IS NEARSIGHTED AND BLIND, AND HAS FORGOTTEN THAT HE HAS BEEN CLEANSED FROM HIS PAST SINS.

Take five minutes to meditate on this Scripture. This different level of Christianity is supposed to be typical Christianity. It is sad to say that too few Christians are at that level. But God is looking to build that level into a new army of young believers. Having character in your life distinguishes you from those who are going up and down, back and forth in their walk with God. It's not driven by emotions, concerts, or activities. It's driven by a passion for God and a commitment to build godly habits into your life. Committing to the ten challenges puts you at a different level of Christianity because you are determined to live up to a higher standard. Things that others presume are acceptable, you don't. Building character into your life is going to give you the foundation to live the ten challenges.

Living the ten challenges is not just a matter of following a bunch of rules. It's a matter of passionately going after God and doing things that back up that passion. The character traits you will learn about in this devotional will be the muscle required to live the ten challenges. Just as you would have to do with any muscle in your body, you are going to have to work at developing it. You're going to have to renew your mind and focus on building your character just as a bodybuilder focuses on building his body, toning specific muscles in turn to define them and make them grow. You are going to have to work on these character traits and use them. In the same way you work out your body in order to get it in good shape you are going to have to work on your character to get it in good shape.

Too few people have a well-defined character. Many are just a hodgepodge of the neat little things they were before they got saved, but maybe a little better. As a WorldChanger, you've got to passionately go after building and adding things that create an incredible mixture of godly habits. When people look at you, they should see a shining example of what God wants Christians to be.

As you go through the rest of this devotional book, I want you to com-

MISSIONS IS...
giving people
hope in life.
—April

mit to work out the muscles to build character into your life. In each of the next ten weeks we are going to talk about specific character traits. I am going to ask you to do specific things to work the traits into your life. By the end of each week you will have added a new character trait to your life. I want you to commit right now to work on these different areas of your life. By the time you finish this book, others will say about you, "Truly you do have the mark of a WorldChanger on your life because you have the character of God built into the fiber of who you are."

WEEK 3

Passion
for
God

Challenge 1:

WorldChangers Keep Their Relationship with Jesus Alive
by Keeping Their Quiet Times

Week 3 · DAY 1

The Most Important Thing

MARK 12:28-30
ONE OF THE TEACHERS OF THE LAW CAME AND HEARD THEM DEBATING.
NOTICING THAT JESUS HAD GIVEN THEM A GOOD ANSWER, HE ASKED HIM, "OF
ALL THE COMMANDMENTS, WHICH IS THE MOST IMPORTANT?"

"THE MOST IMPORTANT ONE," ANSWERED JESUS, "IS THIS: 'HEAR, O
ISRAEL, THE LORD OUR GOD, THE LORD IS ONE. LOVE THE LORD YOUR GOD
WITH ALL YOUR HEART AND WITH ALL YOUR SOUL AND WITH ALL YOUR MIND AND
WITH ALL YOUR STRENGTH.'"

Jesus says here that the most important thing is to love the Lord our God with all of our hearts. To be successful in keeping your relationship with Jesus alive and making your quiet times full of life, you have to have a heart that beats for God. Your heart has to be swelled with passion and yearning to love Him more than anything else you ever thought of.

In this passage, Jesus makes it very clear that God wants our hearts. He wants us to wrap our lives around Him. He wants to stir us up, float our boats, grab our hearts! He wants to preoccupy us. He wants us to love Him not just with our heads, not just with words. Many people answer the question, "Do you love God?" with, "Well, sure. I don't hate Him. I love a nice sunny day. I love peanut butter and jelly. I love pizza. And I love God." But Jesus is talking about something much deeper. He says, "I want the very core of your gut. I want you to love the Lord your God with every ounce of passion you can muster."

Stop for a minute right now and tell the Lord that you love Him. Say it out loud—I LOVE YOU, LORD! Now say it again—I LOVE YOU, LORD! Now say it as if you were saying it right at the throne, looking Jesus right in the eye—I LOVE YOU, LORD! Now say it as if you were looking at Him on the cross and right before you He is about to die—I LOVE YOU, LORD! Now imagine yourself walking down your high school hallway—I LOVE YOU, LORD! Whispering it during geometry class—I LOVE YOU, LORD! During lunchtime—I LOVE YOU, LORD! During football practice—I LOVE YOU, LORD! Hanging out with your friends (under your breath)—I LOVE YOU, LORD! Today, I want you to practice saying I LOVE YOU, LORD! with all of your gut all day long. I want you to practice loving God and wrapping your entire life around Him all day today, and see how it transforms your life.

Write Mark 12:30 (underlined) on an index card and carry it with you today. Memorize this verse, chew on it, and quote it all day long. Go out and love the Lord today!

With All of Your Heart

MARK 12:29 – 30

"THE MOST IMPORTANT [COMMANDMENT]," ANSWERED JESUS, "IS THIS: 'HEAR O ISRAEL, THE LORD OUR GOD, THE LORD IS ONE. LOVE THE LORD YOUR GOD WITH ALL YOUR HEART AND WITH ALL YOUR SOUL AND WITH ALL YOUR MIND AND WITH ALL YOUR STRENGTH.'"

The phrase "all your heart" is used twenty-three times in the Bible. God is trying to make a point here: He doesn't want you just to follow a bunch of rules and regulations; He wants your heart. He doesn't want you to be like a robot, doing a bunch of things that are written down in a rule book just because you were programmed that way. He wants a relationship. He wants a heart-to-heart linkup with you. He wants to be knit together at the heart with you.

What do you think it means to have your heart knit with God's?

_____

_____

_____

We human beings always try to reduce our relationship with God to a bunch of rules. I think that is why a lot of people don't become Christians—they think Christianity is just a bunch of rules. They think, *God will ruin my fun. I will have to follow all of these rules*.

God has never been into a bunch of rules. He has always been into people's hearts. In fact, the first four commandments have to do with a relationship with Him—honoring Him, having no other gods before Him, setting a whole day aside to worship Him and love Him.

EXODUS 20:3–10
YOU SHALL HAVE NO OTHER GODS BEFORE ME. YOU SHALL NOT MAKE FOR YOURSELF AN IDOL IN THE FORM OF ANYTHING IN HEAVEN ABOVE OR ON THE EARTH BENEATH OR IN THE WATERS BELOW. YOU SHALL NOT BOW DOWN TO THEM OR WORSHIP THEM; FOR I, THE LORD YOUR GOD, AM A JEALOUS GOD, PUNISHING THE CHILDREN FOR THE SIN OF THE FATHERS TO THE THIRD AND FOURTH GENERATION OF THOSE WHO HATE ME, BUT SHOWING LOVE TO A THOUSAND GENERATIONS OF THOSE WHO LOVE ME AND KEEP MY COMMANDMENTS. YOU SHALL NOT MISUSE THE NAME OF THE LORD YOUR GOD, FOR THE LORD WILL NOT HOLD ANYONE GUILTLESS WHO MISUSES HIS NAME. REMEMBER THE SABBATH DAY BY KEEPING IT HOLY. SIX DAYS YOU SHALL LABOR AND DO ALL YOUR WORK, BUT THE SEVENTH DAY IS A SABBATH TO THE LORD YOUR GOD.

It seems that it is easier for us to reduce our relationship with God to a bunch of rules. We think if we just abide by the rules, then we won't have to get into heart issues. The heart issues, although sometimes difficult to deal with, bring us freedom when Jesus really comes in and melts and changes our hearts.

If you are going to keep your relationship with Jesus alive, you have to stay connected to Him heart to heart. You have to let Him fill your heart. You have to long for Him with all your heart all day long today. You have to dive into the Scripture and say, "God, fill my heart with Your Word today." You have to have a passionate desire to grab hold of Him right now more than you ever have in your life. You have to let your heart scream as loud as you can, "Lord God, I want You with ALL OF MY HEART,

MISSIONS HAS GIVEN ME... hope for our generation.
—Tim

and I love You with ALL OF MY HEART! Now speak to me, Lord."

Jesus didn't want this to be a flippant, casual desire: "Oh, Lord, I sort of want You." He says you have to love Him with all of your heart. Many times Jesus said things like "he who has ears to hear, let him hear" as He was getting ready to share a parable. He was saying, "Listen, if you want this thing, you've got to really listen. Not everyone who has ears is going to really hear this thing. You've got to really want it." It is the same way with love for God. If you are just going through the motions and saying the rhetoric with your lips, then it doesn't mean anything. He wants more than just the kind of love that you have for pizza, the kind of love that you have for peanut butter and jelly. He wants you to love Him with all of your heart.

This morning and every morning,* start off your quiet time and your day by saying, "Lord, I love You with all of my heart. Now fill me up today as I read Your Word." Then dive in, read some Scripture, and let Him fill you. Make sure you stay in a relationship with Jesus today, and don't just try to follow the rules.

*Many people have quiet time in the morning, but you can have it any time during the day.

Don't Let the World Kidnap Your Passion

PSALM 119:148
MY EYES STAY OPEN THROUGH THE WATCHES OF THE NIGHT,
THAT I MAY MEDITATE ON YOUR PROMISES.

It seems that the world is bent on stealing our passion. We are talking this week about having a passion for God where He captures our attention, our imagination, and our hearts. The devil is constantly putting things before us to lure us away from God. He wants to capture our attention. He wants to capture our passion with fake substitutes that lead nowhere.

Some people have a passion for sports. They think about it, they watch it, they play it, and they look at statistics and magazines. Sports, sports, sports—it's always on their minds.

Other people have a passion for movies, video games, music, concerts, or music videos. And still other people have a passion for a guy or girl. That is probably the most common passion.

The *Webster's New Collegiate Dictionary* definition of *passion* is "an intense emotion compelling action; any object of desire or deep interest." Jesus wants to be the strong desire in our lives. The world offers us many things as objects of that strong desire. The tragedy is that too many people who sit in church every week call themselves Christians, but their passions are for things in the world. They say they love God, but they can't wait to leave church so they can do something that they really enjoy.

Jesus wants to be the object of our PASSION. He wants to be what we dream about when we go to sleep at night. When our passion is for Jesus, we can't wait to get up so that we can serve Him and get closer to Him. We stay awake thinking about Him all night, just as David talked about in the verse today.

List some things that have been the object of your passion.

Too many people who call themselves Christians are walking around in a trance, hypnotized by the world, having a passion for things that are lifeless.

Today, I want you to take some time to ask God to forgive you for having other things as the objects of your passion. Begin to focus your heart, your energy, and your strong desire after the things of God.

Pray,

Lord, forgive me for having these things as the objects of my passion. Only You should be the object of my passion. Today, I set You in the center of my passion that my heart would reach toward You all day long.

Memorize Psalm 119:148. Think about it all day.

Jesus' Lordship: A New Boss

LUKE 6:46
WHY DO YOU CALL ME, "LORD, LORD," AND DO NOT DO WHAT I SAY?

What does "Jesus is Lord" really mean? A lot of people call Jesus "Lord." A lot of people say that Jesus is their boss. But if you call Him a boss, don't you have to do what He says? Calling Jesus your Lord or your boss is not the same as having a boss that you are forced to do things for because you get paid. God wants you to willingly submit all of your life to Him because you love Him more than anything else. He wants you to come after Him with all your heart. He doesn't want to have to continually rebuke you, telling you what to do and bossing you around all day. Instead you are to be running back to wrap your life around Him continually and submit to Him.

Becoming a Christian is a lot like joining the army, except more intense. When you say that you give your life to Jesus and acknowledge His lordship, it means you belong to Him. It means He is the boss. It means He is in charge. Paul often said in his letters that we don't belong to ourselves anymore; we belong to

God. If we belong to God, then He has the right to tell us to do whatever He wants us to do.

Now remember, it is not because Jesus is into rules; it is because we have given our hearts to Him that we choose to serve. We can come after Him every day with that kind of heart and willingly submit our lives to Him. Then we begin to discover the essence of real joy and real life. Jesus doesn't want just our outward obedience; He wants our hearts submitted to Him. He wants to rule our motives. He wants to be in charge of our emotions, our desires, and our innermost beings.

One way you keep your relationship alive every day is to come running back to Him in your prayer time every day. Keep asking Him, "Lord, is there anything in my life that is causing a wall between You and me? I love You so much I don't want that wall there." Then stop and listen, and wait for Him to speak to you. When you hear Him tell you what that thing is, ask Him to forgive you. Find a Scripture that deals with that issue, and repent right away. When you do, you'll feel the life of Jesus flood you that very day. You'll feel His love flood your heart, and you can respond by grabbing hold of Him afresh and anew. In fact, why don't you stop right now and ask Him if there is anything between you? Write the response here.

 Now take some time to ask Him to forgive you. Repent and ask Him to fill your life all over with His love. Then reaffirm your passion and your love for Him.

Rules Versus Relationship

MARK 10:21
JESUS LOOKED AT HIM AND LOVED HIM. "ONE THING YOU LACK," HE SAID.
"GO, SELL EVERYTHING YOU HAVE AND GIVE TO THE POOR, AND YOU WILL HAVE
TREASURE IN HEAVEN. THEN COME, FOLLOW ME."

We're talking about having a passion for God—a yearning and a heart beating to know Him more than anything else. A heart that is crying out, "God, I love You and
nothing else is even a close second." Jesus told a story about a
guy who needed a passion like this. In Mark 10:17–22, He told
the story about a rich young ruler. Turn in your Bible right now
and read this passage.

Jesus was trying to get into the heart of this young man who
had a lot of money, who thought he had his act together but still
felt empty. He came to Jesus and said, "Lord, what must I do to
have eternal life?" He thought that having eternal life had to do
with what he did. Like many of us, he thought, *If I can just do
something good, if I can obey some rule, then I can make it into*

heaven by completing the right list of rules. But Jesus wasn't—and isn't—into rules; He was—and is—into relationships.

Jesus used this conversation to try to help this man understand what was going on. He said, "Okay, you like rules. Try these rules," and He listed six commandments. The young man said, "I've been doing all of these commands and rules since I was a boy." In other words, he said, "I've been a good little youth group kid. I've been doing all of the things that I'm supposed to do to look spiritual, but I still feel empty. What's wrong?" Many young people in youth groups today feel the same way. They've been doing everything that looks right and spiritual on the outside, yet they still feel empty on the inside. They're crying out, "What's wrong?"

Jesus told this man that the core of his problem wasn't that he didn't have enough rules to follow but that his heart was not in the right position. The man cried out, "Doing all of these things, what do I still lack?" A lot of young people are saying the same things in youth groups all across the country: "What do I still lack? Why am I still dry? Why do I still feel empty? I've been doing all the spiritual things and everybody thinks I'm so spiritual, but I still feel dry." Jesus said, "One thing you lack. Go, sell everything you have." He was saying to the man that his problem wasn't in the things that he was doing; it was where his heart was. He had something in his heart that he loved more than he loved God. That was the problem.

In this man's case it was money; what is it in yours? YOU NEED TO GET RID OF WHATEVER YOU LOVE MORE THAN GOD. You need to rip it out of your heart. You need to trash it and throw it away. Jesus said, "Go, sell everything you have and give to the poor. Then you'll have treasure in heaven."

This is the problem of too many young people in church today. They look spiritual on the outside, but they feel dry on the inside because they love a bunch of other things besides God. They say with their lips that they love God, but the passion in their hearts is beating for something else besides the Lord.

The Bible says that this young man went away sad and empty

because he had many rich and valuable things that he felt he could never get rid of. To keep your passion for God alive, you need to make sure that there is nothing in your heart that you love more than Him.

 Take some time right now and look at your heart. Ask yourself honestly if there is anything you love more than Jesus. If so, take some time to rip it out of your heart and repent. If it means you need to throw some of these things away—whether that means CD's, clothes, or whatever you might love more than Him—throw them away and let Him be the object of your affection today. Do you have friendships that draw your attention away from God? You may need to break off those friendships as soon as possible to get free from ungodly influences.

Write down anything you had to repent of.

_____

_____

_____

Make a habit of examining your heart to make sure nothing is in there that you love more than you love Jesus.

The Josiah Thing

Amos 5:15
Hate evil, love good,
   Maintain justice in the courts.
Perhaps the Lord God Almighty will have mercy
   on the remnant of Joseph.

W e're going to look at another example of a young man who had the opportunity to have his love for God directed in the right way. His name was Josiah. He became king when he was eight years old. When he got older, he decided to have the temple cleaned out because it was a mess. When he sent the priests in to clean out the temple, they found the Scriptures that hadn't been read in years. In 2 Kings 23, you can read what happened. I want you to turn in your Bible right now and read verses 2 through 25.

As you can see from this account, Josiah was quite a radical. The priests found the Book of the Law and read it. After they read it, Josiah radically recommitted his heart to the Lord. He decided to go ballistic for God. All of a sudden, his heart started beating with such a passion for the Lord that he ruthlessly began to destroy anything that got between him and God or between any of the people and God. Josiah removed articles in the temple that were dedicated to Baal, the demonic god. He burned them outside the city. He tore down the Asherah pole, which was another demonic god, and ground it to powder (v. 6). He tore down the living quarters of the male prostitutes (v. 7). Can you believe they actually had prostitutes in the temple?

This guy was going crazy! He pulled down altars that had been built to false gods (v. 12). He smashed sacred demonic stones that were carved in different shapes (v. 14). He demolished high places where they sacrificed to demonic gods (vv. 13–15). He slaughtered the priests who were dedicated to false gods (v. 20). He got rid of the mediums and spiritists, the household gods, the idols, and all the other detestable things in Judah (v. 24). Josiah's heart was beating so hard for God, he began to rip and thrash and trash anything that looked ungodly wherever he turned.

Some young people say that it is too hard to live for the Lord and to resist temptation. But I say it is hard only if you don't have a heart after God. Amos 5:15 says that you should love good and hate evil. You are not to love this world or anything of this world. And 1 John 2:15 says that it is hard to live for God only if you love the things of this world. But if you love God and hate what is evil and your heart is beating passionately for God, you want to get away from everything that is evil. It is a lot easier to live for the Lord then.

The Bible says that Josiah turned to the Lord "with all his heart and with all his soul and with all his strength" (2 Kings 23:25). This is what somebody with a passion burning for God in his heart looks like. He hates what is evil and rips it out

MISSIONS IS...
changing people's hearts
and thus changing
a little bit of the world.
—Bethany

of his life wherever he turns, wherever he sees it. A lot of young people wonder why their quiet times dry up with God. Many times they have allowed bits of garbage into their lives and they don't hate evil anymore. They think the evil things are bad, but they don't really hate them.

I want to encourage you to identify some things right now that you have allowed into your life—things that you know are bad but you don't really hate. Take the time now to list them right here.

Make a decision to hate these things, to turn away from them, to repent from them, and then to wrap your life around God. Go after Him with so much passion and fervor that you leave these things in the dust. These things are not sort of bad; they're either really right or really wrong. As you make a decision to hate evil and love good, your passion for God will swell in your heart.

Take the time to memorize Amos 5:15, and carry it with you all day long today.

Week **3**

DAY 7

Keeping Him First

REVELATION 2:2 – 4

I KNOW YOUR DEEDS, YOUR HARD WORK AND YOUR PERSEVERANCE. I KNOW THAT YOU CANNOT TOLERATE WICKED MEN, THAT YOU HAVE TESTED THOSE WHO CLAIM TO BE APOSTLES BUT ARE NOT, AND HAVE FOUND THEM FALSE. YOU HAVE PERSEVERED AND HAVE ENDURED HARDSHIPS FOR MY NAME, AND HAVE NOT GROWN WEARY. YET I HOLD THIS AGAINST YOU: YOU HAVE FORSAKEN YOUR FIRST LOVE.

Take five minutes right now and repeat Revelation 2:2–4 over and over again until you have memorized it. What is the first love that God is talking about here?

_____

_____

_____

God is talking about people who had done great things for Him. They worked hard and persevered. But in the midst of all that, they somehow lost their first love. It seems that too many people like that go to church every week—they do all of the spiritual-looking things, wear Christian shirts, and scream JESUS really loud at concerts. They go to all the Christian activities, sleepovers, and summer camps, but many have lost their first love. Their passion for the Lord is gone.

As a WorldChanger, you need to be known as someone who has a passion for God. When others walk away from you, they might not know much about you, but one thing they should know is that you have a passionate, fervent, fiery love for God that will not quit. You don't want them just to see a bunch of things that you have done for God. You want them to see that you really are connected, that He really is your priority.

This whole week we have been talking about having a passion for God. This will be a week that you will want to keep coming back to again and again. If you don't have a passion for the Lord, all of the rest of this book and the ten challenges are just a bunch of words—rules and regulations. These challenges were never meant to be another list of things that you have to do. They are a way of making the reality of your love for God practical.

If you have gotten into the work scheme and you are working hard doing lots of things but you have lost your first love, right now is the time to slam on your brakes and get your priorities right. It is time to stop doing and doing. It's time to start listening and hearing His voice. It's time to let Him melt your heart once again. Feel the forgiveness of Jesus washing your sin away, just as you felt it the first time you asked Him to come and live inside you. Feel the freedom that He gives you as you sit there and ask Him to fill you with His love.

Meditate on Revelation 2:2–4 so that it will guard your heart and keep you from ever losing your first love. We are not just an army of people busy doing stuff for God. We are an army of people wrapped up with a love and a passion for Him that won't quit.

WEEK 4

Stability

Challenge 2:
WorldChangers Commit Their Mind to God

What Is Stability?

1 TIMOTHY 4:12
DON'T LET ANYONE LOOK DOWN ON YOU BECAUSE YOU ARE YOUNG, BUT SET AN
EXAMPLE FOR THE BELIEVERS IN SPEECH, IN LIFE, IN LOVE, IN FAITH AND IN PURITY.

Take four minutes to memorize this verse. Say it over and over again. You have probably heard this verse many times. We are going to talk about it today as we begin to think about what it means to have stability in your walk with Christ. There are too many young people who are on a Christian roller coaster. If they are at a concert with a bunch of other wild teenagers for the Lord, then they will be excited. But if they are the only ones at school who are Christians, they get depressed. It's just a hype-oriented Christianity.

I am going to tell you right now that God is not into hype. He is into stability. He is into men and women who are going to put their feet on the solid rock of Jesus and keep growing. It doesn't matter how young you are. He wants you to have that kind of stability in your life.

In 1 Timothy, Paul talks about being stable. He says don't let anyone look down on your youth. You know why? Because many adults look down on teenage Christians because they *are* so driven by hype and emotions. They are up one week and down another. They go to

MISSIONS HAS GIVEN ME... the knowledge of a real relationship with God, knowing that I was created to love Him, not to work for Him.
—Alicia

camp, and they are on fire. Two weeks later they're living in sin. Back and forth, back and forth. These adults mock teenagers' Christianity because they think it's just one hype after another.

You need to start blowing them away with your stability. Paul says not to dare let anyone mock you. In fact, be an example to others in all these different areas: speech, life, love, faith, and purity. Most of the time we look at adults as examples, but Paul admonished Timothy, a young guy, to be an example. Paul told him to show them what it was like to really love and have a godly, pure life.

When people look at you, a young person, they should be blown away and say, "Wow! I've never seen anybody with such a pure heart, such a pure life, such pure motives. I've never seen anybody who is so stable and regular—always loving God and having quiet times." You need to show the adults in your church, including your parents and pastors, an example of stability. As you prove to have a stable life and show an example of stability, you will shut the mouth of every mocker. How can people mock somebody who is living such a stable life? How can they mock you when you do what you said you would do?

List some areas where you could be an example for your parents starting right away.

Make this the prayer of your heart today and all week long:

 Lord Jesus, more than anything I want to have a stable walk with You. I am tired of hype-oriented Christianity. I want to get off the spiritual roller coaster. I want to plant my feet on solid ground and grow up as a person of God. I purpose in my heart to be stable in my walk with You today and every day. In Jesus' name, amen.

Meditate on 1 Timothy 4:12 all day long today.

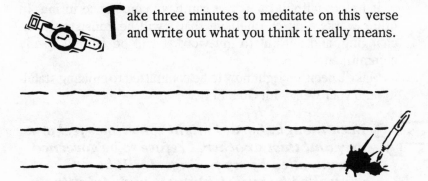

Sticking with It

PROVERBS 20:6
MANY A MAN CLAIMS TO HAVE UNFAILING LOVE,
BUT A FAITHFUL MAN WHO CAN FIND?

Take three minutes to meditate on this verse and write out what you think it really means.

This week we are talking about stability in your walk with God. Stability in your walk with God is directly linked to challenge 2: WorldChangers commit their mind to God. The mind is the battlefield for the devil. If you win the battle in your mind, then you win it in life. And when the devil can flip your mind out going back and forth with temptations, sin, or whatever, then he'll keep you going up and down, back and forth as a Christian. If you're going to be stable in your walk with God, you have to commit your mind to Him.

Proverbs 20:6 talks about being faithful. Faithfulness is a characteristic of stability. You hear a lot of people say, "I am going to love you. I am going to be there for you." But not enough people are actually faithful. A lot of people go forward at conferences and camps to give their lives to Jesus. They say, "Lord, I am going to love You. Lord, I am going to live for You." But not nearly as many stay faithful. Being faithful means doing what you said you would do. Being faithful means others can believe that you are going to be consistent. You are going to do the things that you always do. And the things that you are in the habit of doing are the right things.

The Scripture emphasizes that God doesn't care as much about what you say. He cares about your faithfulness and stability. He cares about your faithfulness to Him, to your own word, and to other people.

If I am a faithful man, you can have confidence in me. In other words, you can believe that I will be consistent, unchanging, and faithful to my word. I will be faithful to my commitments.

Make a decision right now to be committed to building stability into your walk with God. Pray,

Even though, Lord, I might sometimes feel one way and then another, I refuse to be governed or controlled by my feelings. I will be controlled by my faithfulness and stability. In Jesus' name, amen.

Benefits of Stability

PROVERBS 28:20
A FAITHFUL MAN WILL BE RICHLY BLESSED,
BUT ONE EAGER TO GET RICH WILL NOT GO UNPUNISHED.

Y ou can see the promise here that if you have stability and faithfulness, God will richly bless you. Let me tell you how. First, when you become faithful, you become more like the Father. Psalms says over and over again how faithful God is. He is always faithful, faithful, faithful. And when you become faithful, you become like Him. And the more you become like Him, the more excited He gets and so the more He blesses you. So supernaturally, blessing is attracted to you.

Many people pray, "God, please bless me. Please. Please. Please." But the fact is that if you line your life up according to His principles and build character into your life, His blessing is promised to come your way. You didn't even have to pray for it. You can pray, but it's going to come your way anyway because that's the kind of God He is. I think we'd all be better off if we did less begging for blessing and more practicing of God's character in our lives so God's blessing will be drawn to us.

Second, when you build faithfulness and stability into your life, even in the natural realm blessing is drawn toward you. What do I mean? When people see that they can count on you, that you're stable in all your ways, they will trust you with more. You'll get promoted into leadership. You'll get promoted in your job. You'll get more responsibility. Your youth pastor might let you share in a meeting. You might get elected to a position in student government.

Blessing comes your way, even in the natural realm, when you build stability into your life. For example, let's say you want

MISSIONS HAS GIVEN ME...
purpose
and direction.
—Christa

to take out a loan to buy a house. The banker will look at your stability. How long have you lived in your current house? How long did you live in the house before that? How long have you had your job? When the banker sees that you have proven stability, she is willing to loan you money.

Here's another example of natural blessings that come from having stability. Maybe you're wondering why you haven't received a promotion, or why your parents won't trust you with certain things, or why you haven't had the opportunity to do the things you wanted. Well, if your authority figures look in your life and see a lack of stability, they'll have a lack of trust. But when you build stability and faithfulness in your life, people in leadership positions feel free to trust you.

List some areas of your life in which you would like to be more stable.

_____

_____

_____

What can you do to show more stability in these areas?

_____

_____

_____

Do these things today.

If you want God's blessing on your life, start showing some faithfulness and stability. You'll be amazed at what will happen naturally and supernaturally as people start believing in you, counting on you, and giving you more opportunity. Doors will open all around you as you begin to prove your faithfulness. Think about what you could do today to demonstrate faithfulness and stability in your life.

Meditate on Proverbs 28:20 all day long today.

It Keeps Your Head Cool

JAMES 1:19
MY DEAR BROTHERS, TAKE NOTE OF THIS: EVERYONE SHOULD BE QUICK TO
LISTEN, SLOW TO SPEAK AND SLOW TO BECOME ANGRY.

Stability can reach into a number of areas in our lives. We do a number of things that very quickly demonstrate whether we're stable or faithful or not. James talks about being quick to listen, slow to speak, and slow to anger. Many people are quick to speak and quick to get angry, but they hardly ever listen.

Having stability in your character will affect the way you listen to people. It will affect how quick you are to speak and to become angry. Let me put it simply. If you're blowing up all the time and getting hacked off at people, then others won't see you as stable. They will not know whether they can count on you, and they will assume they cannot. They'll never know if they are going to push the wrong button and cause you to explode. That's not exactly the kind of personality that exudes stability.

We all know people who are so hotheaded that they're totally unpredictable. We are always afraid to be ourselves around them. We feel that we have to walk on eggshells because we are afraid of getting our heads bitten off. That's not stability. Some people too easily get in a bad mood. We don't know what might cause them to get depressed and so we're always gun-shy around them. That's not stability, either.

Stability is demonstrated in the way you listen, in the way you talk, and in your temperament. You need to exude stability in everything you say and do. People should know that it's very hard to set you off or provoke you because you've chosen to be stable in all your ways. You've chosen to be quick to listen instead of quick to anger. You would rather sit down and listen to the whole thing before you react.

This is something you are going to have to practice. You can start practicing it today. I want you to take James 1:19 with you and meditate on it all day long. I mean chew on it and chew on it so in every situation you are somebody who is quick to listen. You don't respond without thinking; you don't shoot off your mouth or get angry. You stop and listen. Get serious with it today.

Go back and look at the list you made yesterday. Could you work on some area today that ties in with James 1:19? Write it here.

Purpose now in your heart to listen to the whole situation before you respond at all. And when you respond, respond calmly. Practice it today, and see how God's blessing will touch your life as a result.

Holding Your Tongue

JAMES 1:26

IF ANYONE AMONG YOU THINKS HE IS RELIGIOUS, AND DOES NOT BRIDLE HIS TONGUE BUT DECEIVES HIS OWN HEART, THIS ONE'S RELIGION IS USELESS (NKJV).

We are talking about stability, being somebody who is faithful, somebody who is the same all the time. Does that mean you are a boring person? No, it's the very opposite. It means that you are taking on the personality and character of Jesus and that people can count on you to be consistent. We talked yesterday about being stable in the way you listen, speak, and respond. We are going to talk a little bit more about speech today.

Write out what you think James 1:26 means for you today.

James talks about bridling your tongue, about being someone who doesn't say *everything* you think. If you are going to be stable, you have to control your thoughts. You have to learn to screen your thoughts so that everything you think doesn't automatically come out of your mouth. You need to cast down some thoughts. You need to rebuke some thoughts. You need to keep some thoughts to yourself.

Some people, under the guise of honesty, share everything that comes to their brains, and as a result they often hurt people's feelings. They say a lot of things that communicate instability. They have no screening mechanism. You need to make sure that your screening mechanism for what you say is that you will say only what is edifying to somebody else (see Eph. 4:29).

Faithfulness is reflected in your commitments and in the way you talk. It's amazing—you can say everything you want about how committed you are to the Lord, but ripping people down even once will immediately communicate instability. No one will believe any of your talk of commitment. People judge you by how your words line up with your actions. You want them to see stability and character in your life.

 I want to encourage you today to take James 1:26 to heart. Take five minutes right now to memorize it. Write it down on an index card. Take it with you all day.

Be careful today to control your tongue. Provide a straining mechanism in your brain that strains out all the garbage and casts down the worthless thoughts. Only say things that are fruitful and edifying and worthy of praise. Watch the jokes that you tell or listen to. Watch the comments, even the funny ones, that you make about other people. Be careful that you are not cutting others down. Keep your mind on the Word of God, and let that act as a screening mechanism for what you say today.

DAY 6

Stable Faith

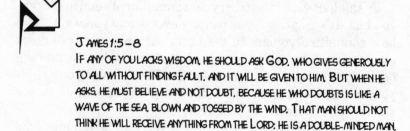

JAMES 1:5-8

IF ANY OF YOU LACKS WISDOM, HE SHOULD ASK GOD, WHO GIVES GENEROUSLY
TO ALL WITHOUT FINDING FAULT, AND IT WILL BE GIVEN TO HIM. BUT WHEN HE
ASKS, HE MUST BELIEVE AND NOT DOUBT, BECAUSE HE WHO DOUBTS IS LIKE A
WAVE OF THE SEA, BLOWN AND TOSSED BY THE WIND. THAT MAN SHOULD NOT
THINK HE WILL RECEIVE ANYTHING FROM THE LORD; HE IS A DOUBLE-MINDED MAN,
UNSTABLE IN ALL HE DOES.

According to this Scripture, what makes a man unstable in all his ways?

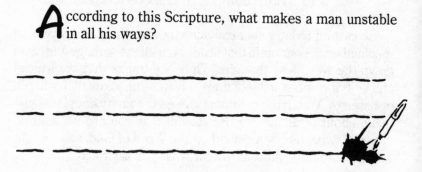

What makes a man unstable in all his ways is wavering faith. James is talking about praying for wisdom, but it applies to anything that you pray for. He says that when you ask, don't you dare doubt.

James says not to doubt or waver because if you do, you'll be tossed around just like a ship in a storm, and that's what too many Christians are like. They wonder why they are not stable. But it all starts when their faith isn't stable. When they ask God for something, they ask with hope instead of with faith. They think it might happen, but they are not really sure. Some people pray to give their lives to the Lord, but they are not really sure they can live for Him. It's like, "Well, I *hope* I can live for You. I *hope* I can be strong." Instead of knowing in Jesus' name they have given their lives to Him and He has come to live inside them, they are afraid to commit to live for Him all of their days. As a result, the Bible says, they are unstable in all their ways.

You know, maybe you need to quit asking God to just make you stable and instead work on getting the recipe for stability. The recipe for stability is having confidence in what you've asked God for. From the very first time you gave Him your life and asked Him for forgive- ness—to everything else that you ask Him for with confidence and convic- tion—you know that He has forgiven you and that He lives inside you and that you belong to Him. You're a child of the most high God. His protection is all around you. His

MISSIONS IS...
more of a lifestyle.
—Cami

anointing is on your life. He has a plan for you to use to change this world.

Knowing that stuff brings stability into your life. You're not just a hokey Christian. You're a Christian who is full of faith and confidence in the Word of God. Having that kind of confidence breeds stability in everything you do. You're not hyped up. You're not whacked out. You're not tossed around like a ship on the ocean. You're stable in all your ways.

It's absolutely imperative that you begin to build stability in your life by keeping your mind on the Word of God and being convinced that it's true. I want you to take these next few Scriptures with you everywhere you go and say them again and again and again until you have confidence and they begin to build stability into your life. Write them out on an index card and take them with you everywhere you go for the next three weeks. Chew on them until they are real to you.

PHILIPPIANS 4:13
I CAN DO EVERYTHING THROUGH HIM WHO GIVES ME STRENGTH.

1 JOHN 1:9
IF WE CONFESS OUR SINS, HE IS FAITHFUL AND JUST AND WILL FORGIVE US OUR SINS AND PURIFY US FROM ALL UNRIGHTEOUSNESS.

2 CORINTHIANS 5:17
IF ANYONE IS IN CHRIST, HE IS A NEW CREATION; THE OLD HAS GONE, THE NEW HAS COME!

The Rewards of Stability

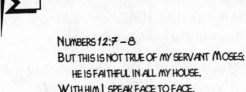

NUMBERS 12:7 – 8
BUT THIS IS NOT TRUE OF MY SERVANT MOSES;
HE IS FAITHFUL IN ALL MY HOUSE.
WITH HIM I SPEAK FACE TO FACE,
CLEARLY AND NOT IN RIDDLES;
HE SEES THE FORM OF THE LORD.

What does this Scripture passage mean to you?

_____

_____

_____

Here you see one of the incredible rewards of stability and faithfulness. The Bible says that Moses was a man who was so faithful that God trusted him to meet with him face-to-face. Can

God say that about you? Do you have much faithfulness? What an incredible thing to happen to Moses. To most people, God spoke through the prophets, and He kept His distance even with them. But Moses was so faithful and so stable that God wanted a personal encounter with him.

Being faithful and stable is *doing what you know is right no matter how you feel*. It's doing what the Word of God says no matter what. Your life is built on something concrete. It was written down by men and inspired by the Holy Spirit. Now you've taken that stability into your heart. You've put your mind to it and decided that no matter how you feel, you're going to do what you know is right. When God sees that kind of seriousness, that kind of stability, in your walk with Him, your intimacy with Him and your ability to hear from Him are going to change. He is going to open up your eyes and show you things you never had a glimpse of before, stuff you never thought a human being could ever know. He did it with Paul. He did it with Moses. And He will do it with you if you prove to have a stable life.

 Father, with all my heart I want to be stable. I commit to build Your Word into my life. I commit to have a strong confidence in Your Word so that I will be stable in all my ways. I commit to do what I know is right and not what I feel because I want to be like You, Lord, and You're so faithful. In Jesus' name, amen.

Write out this week's Scriptures on index cards and carry them with you all day today. Quote them often and meditate on them throughout the day.

WEEK 5

Strength

Challenge 3:

WorldChangers Systematically Study the Bible

Overcoming

> 1 JOHN 2:14
> I WRITE TO YOU, YOUNG MEN,
>   BECAUSE YOU ARE STRONG,
>   AND THE WORD OF GOD LIVES IN YOU,
>   AND YOU HAVE OVERCOME THE EVIL ONE.

The character trait that we are talking about this week is strength. We're talking about having strength in your walk with God. For too long, young people have been blown over by any little temptation that has come their way. It's time to get up and start being strong.

Take five minutes and memorize this Scripture right now.

John is writing to young men who are strong. They are strong because the Word of God lives in them. The caliber of this character trait is directly related to the time that a person spends studying the Word of God. It is directly linked to the third challenge of a WorldChanger: WorldChangers systematically study the Bible.

Many young people are crying out, "Lord, I want to be strong; Lord, I want to be strong," but they never spend time in the Word. They never spend time meditating. They never spend time studying and really learning what the Bible is all about. Then they wonder why they feel so weak.

But God is looking for young men and women who will put their feet on the ground and start being strong. He is looking for people who will quit being kicked around by the world.

John was commenting to the young men. He said, "You have overcome the evil one." He was telling them that they had put so much of the Word of God in themselves that they had overcome. The same can be true of you. It is time for you to stop being overcome by the world and to start overcoming the world because you have so much of the Word of God in you.

God is looking for young people with a blazing fire in their hearts. He doesn't want hype. He doesn't want goose bumps. He wants a commitment and strength. Strength comes from your going back to the Lord and studying the Word of God and meditating on the Word of God every day.

Pray this prayer:

Lord Jesus, I want to be a strong man (or woman) of God. I don't just want to hope to make it; I want to have godly strength and resilience that will stand no matter what comes my way. In Jesus' name, amen.

Now set a goal for yourself of how much time you'll spend with God each day this week. Write that goal here.

What Is Strength?

ake some time now to read Ephesians 6:10–18 in your Bible. Verse 10 says, "Be strong in the Lord and in his mighty power." The Bible doesn't ask us to please try to be strong if we're having a good day. The Bible is very clear. First of all, it says *be*. It's a commandment. It is not a request; it is an imperative. Listen, we are in a war; you have to be strong. Don't just hope that you get strong; make a decision to be strong.

Jesus wouldn't ask you to do something if He didn't give you the power to do it. God is looking for some men and women who, in the midst of all of the things that the devil is doing all over this globe, will decide to be strong no matter what. God is commanding you to be strong, not suggesting that you be strong. Think about that for a second and chew on it. He says to be strong. You have to tell yourself to be strong today, to quit being a wimp and quit being weak. You have to be strong.

The second word here is *strong*. That doesn't mean be a little bit less weak—it means be strong. This Christian walk is not about trying to look through your days and see if you can make it (barely) without letting the devil run over your head. It's about getting the strength of God's Word so established in your heart that when you blast out of your quiet times, you'll be ready for anything the devil throws your way.

Describe one area where you can work on becoming strong beginning today.

I want you to take five minutes right now to memorize verses 10 and 11 of Ephesians 6. Meditate on this Scripture all day long. Write it out on an index card, and take it with you wherever you go today and this week.

It is time to build strength into your life. Begin to see yourself as a man or woman of strong character. When the devil looks at you, he will run because he sees you with the inner strength of the Lord Jesus Christ in your life.

MISSIONS HAS GIVEN ME...
perseverance.
—Amy

All Things

PHILIPPIANS 4:13
I CAN DO EVERYTHING THROUGH HIM WHO GIVES ME STRENGTH.

Y ou get strength in your life by building yourself in the Word of God. You gain strength by studying God's Word and meditating on it, letting it flow down in your heart. A Scripture like this one in Philippians will help you build strength.

You need to say this Scripture as often as you can. Now write it out in 1990s teenage language.

"I can do everything through him who gives me strength." These simple words will absolutely transform your life if you say them so many times that they explode and come alive inside your heart. This world is trying to tell you that it is stupid to live for God. The devil is trying to tell you that you can't resist peer pressure. Many other voices are trying to tell you that you are going to be a failure and you are never going to make it. In the midst of all that, God is saying, "I believe in you. I can see that you are strong. You are strong and can do all things, not just some things."

It's not that you can sort of do a bunch of things. You can do everything through Christ who strengthens you. You can be strong because you have the strength of Christ. He strengthens you.

That strength becomes stronger and stronger as you meditate and chew on His Word. It's like infusion of power from on high as you chew and chew and chew on the Scripture and all of a sudden it explodes and you feel the fire and the courage and the strength of God well up in your heart. So, you know you can—you really can—do all things through Christ who strengthens you.

Now I want you to list your biggest obstacles, the areas where you feel weakest, right here.

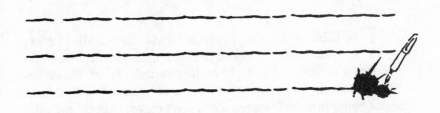

I want you to go through and say this to the Lord and say this to yourself: "I can do (*whatever the weakness is*) _____

as Christ strengthens me." Say that about each of these areas of weakness and leave your quiet time today with confidence, knowing that you can conquer every weakness as Christ gives you strength.

More Than Conquerors

ROMANS 8:37
IN ALL THESE THINGS WE ARE MORE THAN CONQUERORS THROUGH HIM WHO LOVED US.

The Bible is referring to the fact that in the middle of every kind of persecution and circumstance, we are more than conquerors. That means we have the strength of God. This week we are talking about being strong in the Lord. We're talking about being men and women who aren't blown over by any little circumstance.

Find the strength that God put in you when He put His Holy Spirit inside you when you gave your heart to Him. Think about the concept of being more than a conqueror. What do you think it means to be more than a conqueror?

It definitely means that you are not just barely going to make it. It surely doesn't mean that you are struggling to get by as a Christian. A conqueror is somebody who is strong. A conqueror is somebody who is a champion. A conqueror is one who knows he has a strength that will not quit. God is looking to make you into a man or woman of God who has the strength that will not quit. Your strength will endure because you have the strength of the Holy One of Israel.

In spite of everything that the devil has tried to do to keep me from being a successful Christian, I know that my God lives inside me. He is on my side, and He said I'm more than a conqueror. If He said I'm more than a conqueror, then *I know* that I can be more than a conqueror. The key is this: I can't convince you that you are more than a conqueror. You've got to be convinced because *God* says that you are more than a conqueror. God says that you can do all things through Christ.

I want you to take Romans 8:37, write it down on an index card, and carry it around with you all day. I know I've said that before, but you need to do it again today. You need to say it so many times that it is blasting out your brain. You need to say it so many times that God ignites your heart and you're convinced because God has convinced you that you are more than a conqueror. Recite Romans 8:37 so many times that you can blast out of your quiet times and into your school or job today knowing that you can conquer anything that comes your way.

Growing in Strength

LUKE 1:80
AND THE CHILD GREW AND BECAME STRONG IN SPIRIT; AND HE LIVED IN THE
DESERT UNTIL HE APPEARED PUBLICLY TO ISRAEL.

LUKE 2:40
AND THE CHILD GREW AND BECAME STRONG; HE WAS FILLED WITH WISDOM, AND
THE GRACE OF GOD WAS UPON HIM.

Get out your Bible and read around these verses. Who is each verse talking about?

Both John and Jesus had to grow in strength. Strength isn't
something that you just pray for and get right away. You've got to

grow in strength. And you grow by getting the Word of God planted deep in your heart. Even Jesus, the Son of God, grew in strength.

Growing in strength is a process. I want you to make a commitment this week that strength is a character trait you're going to work on for the rest of your life. Then when people look at you, they'll see a person of strength. Your inner person is growing day by day. The same things they said about John, the same things they said about Jesus, they'll say about you. They'll say, "I know this guy and every time I see him, he gets stronger and stronger and stronger. Every time I see him face a temptation, he has a story about how he defeated it because he is growing in strength."

List some areas in which you'd like to grow in strength.

Now begin to pray over these areas. Ask God for some specific Scriptures on how you can get strong in each of these areas.

Begin to quote Luke 1:80 and 2:40. Memorize them and make a commitment today. Say,

Lord, no matter what happens, I'm going to grow in my strength. I want to be like John. I want to be like Jesus. I want the strength I have today to not be the ultimate strength that I will ever have. Let it be just a building block for more strength that I will get tomorrow and the next day because I'm choosing to plant Your Word in my life. In Jesus' name, amen.

I Am Strong!

2 CORINTHIANS 12:10
THAT IS WHY, FOR CHRIST'S SAKE, I DELIGHT IN WEAKNESSES, IN INSULTS, IN HARDSHIPS, IN PERSECUTIONS, IN DIFFICULTIES. FOR WHEN I AM WEAK, THEN I AM STRONG.

JOEL 3:10
BEAT YOUR PLOWSHARES INTO SWORDS
    AND YOUR PRUNING HOOKS INTO SPEARS.
LET THE WEAKLING SAY,
    "I AM STRONG!"

These Scriptures show what happens in the lives of believers when they get hold of the Word of God. Paul says, "I glory in my weaknesses because these are the areas that God has now made strong in me." Some people feel that an area they've been weak in their whole lives is an area they're going to be weak in for the rest of their lives. That's a lie from the pit of hell. God wants to face the devil in a big way in your life by making you strong in areas of weakness. Paul says, "I love to brag about my weak areas because these are the areas that are becoming my strong areas."

Joel tells people who are weak to start saying they're strong! God is going to blast the weak areas out of your life and make them into areas of strength. I want you to take this verse in Joel and use it today to blast your weak areas.

Some of us walk through our Christian lives feeling that we're barely going to make it. We often feel weak and never feel very strong. Too many Christians have a woe-is-me attitude. Too many Christians never realize that the very reason Jesus died was because He was tired of our feeling so weak spiritually and that the flesh is always overcoming us. We, even the weak among us, need to start saying that we're strong in Jesus' name!

It's time to get sick and tired of letting the devil run all over our heads. We need to determine that we will get in the Word and we will get strong. We know the power of God is in His Word, and when we drive the Word into our hearts and lives, we get strong in Jesus' name.

As you take on this challenge of a WorldChanger, to study the Word of God, you'll develop strength, and as you develop strength, you'll have more passion to get back into the Word of God. The stronger you get, the more you want the Word. And the more you get into the Word, the stronger you'll get.

Write out 2 Corinthians 12:10. Begin to confess it and quote it every time you feel weak today. Confess it over any area in your life where you feel weak. Start saying, "I am strong!"

List some areas in which you have felt weak.

Carry today's Scriptures with you. Say them, confess them, and pray them over every area of weakness in your life.

Strength Versus Arrogance

ROMANS 1:30
SLANDERERS, GOD-HATERS, INSOLENT, ARROGANT AND BOASTFUL; THEY INVENT
WAYS OF DOING EVIL; THEY DISOBEY THEIR PARENTS.

ROMANS 11:20
THEY WERE BROKEN OFF BECAUSE OF UNBELIEF, AND YOU STAND BY FAITH. DO
NOT BE ARROGANT, BUT BE AFRAID.

PROVERBS 21:24
THE PROUD AND ARROGANT MAN— "MOCKER" IS HIS NAME;
    HE BEHAVES WITH OVERWEENING PRIDE.

PROVERBS 17:7
ARROGANT LIPS ARE UNSUITED TO A FOOL—
    HOW MUCH WORSE LYING LIPS TO A RULER!

PSALM 5:5
THE ARROGANT CANNOT STAND IN YOUR PRESENCE;
    YOU HATE ALL WHO DO WRONG.

As you can see from these Scriptures, God hates arrogance. I want to warn you that when I talk about being strong in the Lord, I'm not talking about being arrogant. There is a big difference.

Write out what you think is the difference between pride or arrogance (as talked about here) and confidence or strength of character.

As a young Christian, I would see people who thought they were strong in the Lord and they thought that meant being arrogant to everybody. God is not into people having a conceited attitude. A lot of flippant people who call themselves Christians are not very strong in the Lord. They are flippant because of their attitude. They think they know it all. They think they don't really need to take notes in church or listen to other people because they've heard it all before.

Let me warn you: Don't let your strength be interpreted as arrogance. You've got to be convinced through the Word of God that you can do all things through Christ, that you are more than a conqueror, and that nothing is going to slap you upside the head or get you down. But remember that the Bible says, "Pride goes before destruction, and a haughty spirit before a fall" (Prov. 16:18 NKJV), and God hates arrogance. You don't want to get so bigheaded that you think you could never fall.

Stay in the Word of God, and keep studying the Word; that will keep you humble so that you won't fall. You don't want to give people the impression that you think you know it all—that you've been there, that you've done that, and that you know a lot more than anybody else. You want to have the inward confi-

MISSIONS IS...
a new sense
of who I am.
—Candace

dence of knowing there is nothing that the devil could throw at you that you can't overcome. Why? Because you prayed a prayer and asked God for strength? No. It's because every day you're cramming the Word of God down your throat.

This is not something that happens on a onetime basis. It happens over time, just like Jesus and John grew. You're going to have to make a commitment to grow in strength every single day by feeding yourself the Word of God and guarding yourself from arrogance, because as soon as you get into arrogance, you're about ready to take a fall.

I want you to reaffirm your commitment to challenge 3, studying the Word of God. Reaffirm your commitment to have the character trait of strength in your life. When people look at you, they'll see the strength of the living God because you've taken the Word of God and buried it deep in your heart. And with that kind of strength, nothing can knock you over.

WEEK 6

Integrity

Challenge 4:
WorldChangers Have an Accountability Friendship

Week 6

DAY 1

What Is Integrity?

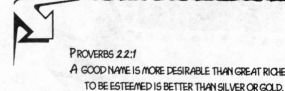

PROVERBS 22:1
A GOOD NAME IS MORE DESIRABLE THAN GREAT RICHES;
TO BE ESTEEMED IS BETTER THAN SILVER OR GOLD.

 I want you to take three minutes right now to memorize this verse and really chew on it. Write out what you think it means.

This week we are talking about integrity. Proverbs 22:1 is essentially about integrity. When you have integrity, you have a good name. You have a strong reputation. You have a name that people associate with something positive because everything you do and say communicates you keep your word.

According to Proverbs 22:1, a good name is more important than silver or gold. Having a good reputation—having integrity, being somebody everybody can count on—is more important than having silver, gold, or anything else you could possibly want in life.

Most of the time our society looks up to you if you can lie and cheat really well. If you can get away with bad things, the world honors you, but the kingdom of God is different. God wants you to have truth in everything you say, everything you do, and everything you're a part of. In God's eyes, the more pure, truthful, and faithful you are, the more honorable you are.

It's time to adopt God's value system. It's time to start valuing a good name and a life full of integrity. Take a moment and list some things here that you think you could do that would give you a good name.

The fourth challenge of a WorldChanger is having an accountability friend, who will help you establish integrity. An accountability partner is somebody you can be completely honest with about everything you're thinking and feeling. An accountability friend will get in your face anytime you look like you're not keeping your word or your name is getting tarnished because you're not representing Christ. Make these words the prayer of your heart today and all week long:

Lord Jesus, please make me a woman (or a man) with a good name. I want to adequately represent You in a way that would honor You. In Jesus' name, amen.

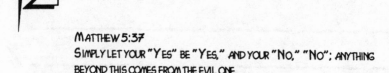

Your Word

MATTHEW 5:37
SIMPLY LET YOUR "YES" BE "YES," AND YOUR "NO," "NO"; ANYTHING
BEYOND THIS COMES FROM THE EVIL ONE.

Being a person of integrity is being someone who means what he says and says what he means. It's being somebody who follows through on what she says she is going to do. It used to be in America that a handshake was as good as a contract. You didn't need a written contract—you just gave your word and shook on it and people could count on you. But today, lawyers draw up all kinds of contracts. You have to read the fine print, sign on the dotted line, and have it notarized. It's become necessary because people can't trust each other to keep their word.

Problems with integrity started way back before Jesus' time. People started swearing by things instead of promising something in their own name: "I swear I'll do this," or "I swear I'll do that," or "I'll swear by heaven this and that." Their name wasn't good enough to put on the line, so they swore by heaven or by hell. Jesus said, "Listen, that's not the kind of people you're supposed to be. Don't swear by heaven or by hell. Be a person who is so full of integrity that people can trust you when you simply say, 'Yes, I'll do it,' or 'No, I won't.'"

Sometimes doing what they say is simply a matter of remembering. Some people give an excuse, "Well, I am sorry. I just forgot to do it," or "I didn't remember that I decided to quit doing that thing." But that's not good enough. People of integrity find a way to remind themselves that they committed to something. When their word, their name, is on the line, they won't do anything to tarnish it.

Sometimes not keeping their word is a matter of deliberately lying or committing to do something that either they have no business completing or they have no way to complete. Some people say yes to a thing, but then when no one is looking, they won't do it.

MISSIONS IS...
having every false
foundation of your life shaken
until you are left
standing on God alone.
—Ragan

People of integrity are the same in private as in public. What others see is what they get. It's not an act that people put on so others will approve. Many people are like this in their Christian lives—they do things to look spiritual in front of others. You can see them shouting and screaming JESUS, acting spiritual, and wearing Christian T-shirts. They are saying, "Yes, I am a Christian. I love God." But they don't have quiet times; in the heart of hearts they think about garbage; they're involved in sin; they are not really crying out for God with all their hearts. They are hypocrites. When people break their integrity, they are hypocrites.

List some situations in which you have broken your word.

_____ _____ _____ _____ _____

_____ _____ _____ _____ _____

_____ _____ _____ _____ _____

What can you do now to correct the wrong that you've done
and to make up for not having kept your word?

_____ _____ _____ _____ _____

_____ _____ _____ _____ _____

_____ _____ _____ _____ _____

The Bible says that when people are repentant, they always
make up for lost time or for bad situations. The Old Testament
says that when you steal, you have to pay back two to seven
times as much as you took. We all know the story of Zacchaeus
and how he repented before Jesus. He said, "Lord, I will pay back
four times as much as I took from anybody I have wronged." So
as a young person pursuing integrity, you need to seek today
how you can make up for commitments that you've broken in
the past. Take action on it today and watch God's blessing start
to come on your life.

God Is Our Example

ISAIAH 45:23
BY MYSELF I HAVE SWORN,
MY MOUTH HAS UTTERED IN ALL INTEGRITY
A WORD THAT WILL NOT BE REVOKED:
BEFORE ME EVERY KNEE WILL BOW;
BY ME EVERY TONGUE WILL SWEAR.

In this Scripture God is helping us understand what integrity is all about by defining it for us and by describing His own integrity. He is giving us His word on something. He is saying, "Listen, let Me tell you the way it is. When I give My word, I never take it back." Isn't it good to know that God never lies? When He says something, you can count on it; you can take it to the bank. He always does what He says He's going to do. In this case He is saying, "Let Me tell you something: One day every knee is going to bow and every tongue is going to confess that Jesus is Lord. I am giving My word on something, and My word will never be revoked. When I say something, it's as good as done."

As Christians, we need to go after the same kind of integrity.

When we say something, it is as good as done. No one should ever have to wonder whether we're going to keep our word or not. When we give our word, we lay our lives, our reputation, and our credibility on the line. Let's not be flipped airheads who say one thing and then do another.

Don't make all kinds of commitments that you can't keep. When you give your word, it should be clear that you are going to keep it. This goes from the smallest things to the biggest things. For example, when you tell somebody you will pray for him, do you really pray for him? Or is it something that you say but don't really mean? When you tell a friend that you're going to be at a meeting, do you actually make it to the meeting on time? When you tell your friend that you're going to meet her at a restaurant, do you actually make it there? It's a matter of keeping your word and deciding what kind of a person you're going to be.

Start practicing integrity by making small commitments and being faithful to every single commitment that you make. Every time you tell somebody you are going to do something, go overboard. If you don't do anything else, make sure that you fulfill the commitment. Watch the confidence you start gaining in your life today.

By the way, what have you done to make up for the times in the past when you haven't kept your word?

Bend over backward today to make up for lost time.

A Pure Heart

1 KINGS 9:4 – 5

AS FOR YOU, IF YOU WALK BEFORE ME IN INTEGRITY OF HEART AND UPRIGHTNESS, AS DAVID YOUR FATHER DID, AND DO ALL I COMMAND AND OBSERVE MY DECREES AND LAWS, I WILL ESTABLISH YOUR ROYAL THRONE OVER ISRAEL FOREVER, AS I PROMISED DAVID YOUR FATHER WHEN I SAID, "YOU SHALL NEVER FAIL TO HAVE A MAN ON THE THRONE OF ISRAEL."

We're talking about integrity this week. We're talking about being a person of your word. I want to encourage you to find someone now if you don't have an accountability friend, an in-your-face friendship. Grab somebody and say, "Listen, I want you to help me keep my heart pure. I want you to help me keep my word. Anytime you see me not living up to what I say I am going to do, whether in my heart for the Lord or in my relationships with other people, I want you to bring it to my attention. I want to always keep my word."

In this passage of Scripture God is making a promise. I want you to rewrite the promise as it applies to you today. He says, "If you _____ and _____, then

MISSIONS IS...
stepping 12,000 miles out
of your comfort zone.
—Chad

I will _____."
He is describing the benefits of having integrity and defining a little bit more clearly what integrity is. God told Solomon what would happen if he would have an integrity of heart like his father, David, had.

Isn't it interesting that integrity is always linked to the heart? If you have a pure heart, a heart after God, then the way you live with integrity will show it. If you don't live with integrity—if you're not the same on the inside as you are on the outside, if you're different in private from what you are in public—then it shows that your heart is not really pure. Over and over again the Bible links integrity to the heart. God calls us to be pure.

Heart and soul, through and through, you need to be consistent. I want to encourage you if you have found areas in your life that have not shown integrity and you have cried out to God for a clean heart just like David did in Psalm 51. Don't be discouraged. It takes practice to build character in your life. You might find areas where you slip up. But the next day you can go back and keep your word more intensely in that specific area. With practice you'll get better and better, and you'll start establishing the habit of always keeping your word whenever you give it.

God Judges Our Hearts

1 CHRONICLES 29:17
I KNOW, MY GOD, THAT YOU TEST THE HEART AND ARE PLEASED WITH INTEGRITY. ALL THESE THINGS HAVE I GIVEN WILLINGLY AND WITH HONEST INTENT. AND NOW I HAVE SEEN WITH JOY HOW WILLINGLY YOUR PEOPLE WHO ARE HERE HAVE GIVEN TO YOU.

PSALM 7:8
THE LORD SHALL JUDGE THE PEOPLES;
JUDGE ME, O LORD, ACCORDING TO MY RIGHTEOUSNESS,
AND ACCORDING TO MY INTEGRITY WITHIN ME (NKJV).

ake three minutes on each of these Scriptures and chew on them. Write out what you think each one means to you.

_____

_____

_____

The first point I want you to see today is that God judges us by our integrity and by how true we are to our word. He wants to know: When we make a commitment to Him, will we really keep our word? When we give our word and make a commitment to somebody else, do we keep that word? God wants people who don't have corrupted hearts, scamming this thing and trying to get away with that. He is looking for a generation He can truly be proud of. He is looking for people who keep their word just as He keeps His word.

In the psalm, David asked God to judge him according to his integrity. David essentially said, "Look at my life, Lord. I have been keeping my word just like I said I would." In 1 Chronicles, David said, "See, You have tested my heart and You are pleased with my integrity."

When you begin to keep your word, God gets really happy. He is so excited and pleased because you've become more like Him. And nothing gets God more excited than watching you become more like Him. That's why He commands blessing toward you.

Integrity pleases God. One of the biggest goals in my life is to make God smile. I believe all of us should desire that above everything else. Just one smile from the awesome living God who created the whole earth is worth a lifetime of passion and labor striving to please Him. Do everything you can today to be a man or woman of integrity and to please God as He looks through you and judges your heart. Then you can say as David said, "You have judged my heart and are pleased with my integrity."

Integrity Is Our Standard

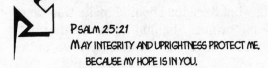

PSALM 25:21
MAY INTEGRITY AND UPRIGHTNESS PROTECT ME,
BECAUSE MY HOPE IS IN YOU.

PROVERBS 11:3
THE INTEGRITY OF THE UPRIGHT GUIDES THEM,
BUT THE UNFAITHFUL ARE DESTROYED BY THEIR DUPLICITY.

PROVERBS 13:6
RIGHTEOUSNESS GUARDS THE MAN OF INTEGRITY,
BUT WICKEDNESS OVERTHROWS THE SINNER.

W hat's the main point that comes through to you in these Scriptures?

_____

_____

_____

We are talking about having integrity and being a person of your word. When you say something, people should be able to bank on it. We have such a huge problem with situational ethics these days that some people don't even know what integrity means. According to situational ethics, whatever feels good at the time is okay to do. It means that I'll judge what's right or wrong whenever I'm in a situation.

The Bible is talking about letting our integrity guide us. In other words, we decide in our hearts that we want to follow God, and we find out what's right. Then we let that standard guide our decisions and not just what seems right at the moment. We base our judgments not on how we feel at the moment, but on what we know is right. We don't have to flip back and forth: "Well, what decision should I make this time? Should I try to sneak out or not? Should I try to cheat or not? Should I keep the extra change that somebody gave me or not?"

When you have integrity, people will be so blown away by your purity and honesty that they'll want to know what you have on the inside. Every day you have to make a thousand decisions—what you're going to wear, what you're going to do, who you're going to hang with. You face peer pressure all the time. God is looking for you to be the kind of person who is guided by integrity. In other words, He, your friends, and even you don't have to wonder what you are going to do in any given situation. You have this confidence because you let the integrity of your heart guide your decisions and not just whatever happens to be popular at that moment.

I want to encourage you right now to think about the commitments you've made to the Lord in the past. Think about your commitment to live with a pure heart, your commitment to be free of sin, and your commitment to follow after Him with all of your heart. Keep the commitments fresh and alive in your heart and mind all day long, and let the commitments guide the decisions you make today.

Security

PROVERBS 10:9
THE MAN OF INTEGRITY WALKS SECURELY,
BUT HE WHO TAKES CROOKED PATHS WILL BE FOUND OUT.

This is probably one of the most incredible advantages of walking with integrity. Please write out what this verse means for you today.

The Bible promises that if you have integrity, you will walk securely. What does that mean? You won't have to worry about the devil picking you off. You won't have to worry about getting stabbed in the back. You won't have to be second-guessing:"Did I tell this lie to one guy and that lie to another person?" Some people have made so many different commitments to so many people and have interwoven so many different lies that they don't know who they've given their word to about what. As a result they never know what's going to come up and bite them.

But the Bible promises that if you walk with integrity, you'll walk securely. People won't be pushing you over; the devil can't knock you down because you're doing what's right. You have a fortress around you, guarding you, protecting you, and strengthening you.

Others can say what they want about you. They can try to hurt you. They can try to tear you down, but nothing will work against you when you have integrity.

Some young people live in fear, wondering what's going to happen to them next, who is going to come after them, or what they're going to be tempted with. The Bible promises that you can blow all that fear out of your brain and mind if you walk with integrity. You'll walk securely; you'll never have to second-guess yourself; you'll never have to wonder about what the future looks like for you. It's going to be secure. It's going to be strong. It's going to be stable because you decided to walk with integrity.

I want to encourage you right now to make integrity a priority in your life. Now that you have read all the Scriptures for the week, make a commitment to memorize them and others.

You have been thinking all week about purposing to make integrity the central part of your life. It's time to decide what kind of person you're going to be. What kind of Christian are you going to be? We talked a little bit about having an accountability friend. If you don't have one, you need to get one now. You need to start sharing your hearts with each other so you can get in each other's face and keep each other accountable. By doing so you keep your integrity at a strong level. Having an accountability friend secures; it's like insurance for maintaining a life of integrity.

WEEK 7

Self-Control

Challenge 5:

WorldChangers Have a Lifestyle of Worship
and Holy Actions

What Is Self-Control?

GENESIS 1:28
GOD BLESSED THEM AND SAID TO THEM, "BE FRUITFUL AND INCREASE IN NUMBER; FILL THE EARTH AND SUBDUE IT. RULE OVER THE FISH OF THE SEA AND THE BIRDS OF THE AIR AND OVER EVERY LIVING CREATURE THAT MOVES ON THE GROUND."

This week we'll talk about having self-control in our lives. We are going to talk about what self-control is, where it comes from, and where it starts. Let me tell you this right now: Self-control is directly linked to challenge 5, which is having a lifestyle of worship and holy actions. If you're going to live a holy life, if you're going to use your energy for holy things, you're going to have to learn self-control, and you're going to have to practice self-control. Character traits may not have exciting names, but they are definitely key to bringing God's blessing on your life.

In Genesis 1:28, we see the very beginning of self-control. God put Adam on the earth. He made all of the trees and animals and put Adam right in the middle of everything. God said, "Adam, you subdue it, you take dominion over it, you take care of it, and you take charge. You are in control of this place." God made us to be people who like to take charge of things. The problem is that *most of us like to take charge of other people instead of taking charge of ourselves*. Adam was commanded to take charge of the whole earth and everything on the earth. The tragedy in the Garden of Eden was Adam's not having self-control and taking dominion over everything on the earth as God told him to do. God gave him the power to dominate, the power to control the animals and himself, and the power to be in charge of this earth.

So our desire to control is good, but we need to focus more on controlling ourselves than on controlling others.

Unfortunately, we have this fleshly sinful nature that wants to control us as well. Adam didn't have it, yet he sinned anyway and he gave us all the sinful nature. The good news is that now we have been redeemed, set free, and given a new heart. We now have the power again to control ourselves and to dominate as God originally intended with Adam.

Some people feel very out of control, as if they just can't help themselves in some areas of their lives. But that's not true; they just *feel* out of control. Are there areas of your life that you feel are out of your control? Write them out here.

As you are going to see this week, God has given us the power to live the self-controlled life so that we can please Him in all we do. I want you to begin to practice today controlling your thoughts and your life and lining them up with the Word of God. See how you can add to that as we progress this week.

What About Drugs and Alcohol?

PROVERBS 20:1

WINE IS A MOCKER AND BEER A BRAWLER;
   WHOEVER IS LED ASTRAY BY THEM IS NOT WISE.

PROVERBS 23:29–35

WHO HAS WOE? WHO HAS SORROW?
   WHO HAS STRIFE? WHO HAS COMPLAINTS?
   WHO HAS NEEDLESS BRUISES? WHO HAS BLOODSHOT EYES?
THOSE WHO LINGER OVER WINE,
   WHO GO TO SAMPLE BOWLS OF MIXED WINE.
DO NOT GAZE AT WINE WHEN IT IS RED,
   WHEN IT SPARKLES IN THE CUP,
   WHEN IT GOES DOWN SMOOTHLY!
IN THE END IT BITES LIKE A SNAKE
   AND POISONS LIKE A VIPER.
YOUR EYES WILL SEE STRANGE SIGHTS
   AND YOUR MIND IMAGINE CONFUSING THINGS.
YOU WILL BE LIKE ONE SLEEPING ON THE HIGH SEAS,
   LYING ON TOP OF THE RIGGING.
"THEY HIT ME," YOU WILL SAY, "BUT I'M NOT HURT!
   THEY BEAT ME, BUT I DON'T FEEL IT!

You might be asking, "What do these Scriptures have to do with self-control?" Maybe you've heard for a long time that it is wrong to drink and do drugs. You've been told that you shouldn't go to parties and get drunk and stuff like that. I would like to share with you the principles behind these rules. Proverbs 20:1 says that wine is a mocker. In other words, when you drink wine or any alcohol, you will be mocked. You will say and do stupid things. You will not be in control of yourself. You might think you are cool when you're drunk or high, but you will be mocked.

Proverbs 23:29–35 talks about the fights that happen when people are drunk. The point here is that as you drink or do drugs, you give your God-given ability to control yourself away to a chemical. So a chemical is in charge of your brain instead of you. A chemical is in charge of your life instead of you. You are no longer responsible because you have artificially induced yourself with something that makes you irresponsible. God created you with something that makes you different from the animals. He gave you the power to dominate this earth and to be in control of your life according to His plan for your life. You have taken that power and reduced it to nothing because when you drink, you give your ability to control yourself over to a drug.

Drugs and alcohol aren't bad just for the sake of being bad. They're bad because the very nature of the human being that God made you

MISSIONS IS...
desperate, hurting, dying
people who need the
pure love of Jesus.
—Curt

with is defiled and blasphemed. Because God created you to be in charge, you mock God's creation when you drink or use drugs. You must learn to have self-control if you are going to live a lifestyle of holy actions. The paradox is that the unholy actions that so many young people are into, drinking and doing drugs, are the very things that give them less self-control. So they sin even more.

If you've been drinking or doing any kind of drugs, I want you to repent right now and ask God to forgive you. Ask Him to forgive you, not just for doing the thing—taking the drug, drinking the alcohol—but for defiling and mocking what He made in you as a human being with the ability to control yourself.

If It Feels Good . . .

2 TIMOTHY 3:1–5

THERE WILL BE TERRIBLE TIMES IN THE LAST DAYS. PEOPLE WILL BE LOVERS OF
THEMSELVES, LOVERS OF MONEY, BOASTFUL, PROUD, ABUSIVE, DISOBEDIENT TO
THEIR PARENTS, UNGRATEFUL, UNHOLY, WITHOUT LOVE, UNFORGIVING,
SLANDEROUS, WITHOUT SELF-CONTROL, BRUTAL, NOT LOVERS OF THE GOOD,
TREACHEROUS, RASH, CONCEITED, LOVERS OF PLEASURE RATHER THAN LOVERS OF
GOD—HAVING A FORM OF GODLINESS BUT DENYING ITS POWER. HAVE NOTHING
TO DO WITH THEM.

Rewrite 2 Timothy 3:1–5 in your own words.

_____

_____

_____

As you can see, this is a progression of what we've already learned. God made people to be in control and to take dominion.

But people have continually given that control away to the sinful nature—to alcohol, drugs, and peer pressure. Now we see a picture of the last days when people will be totally messed up. The crux of it is that they don't have any self-control. They're controlled by all kinds of things outside themselves with no discretion or sense of controlling what they do. If you look around today, you'll see that confusion is rampant among young people in high schools and colleges, even among adults. Some people don't have a clear priority of doing what's right or really taking charge of their lives—they do whatever feels good at the time.

MISSIONS HAS GIVEN ME...
a passion for the world.
—Amanda

Even some Christians fail again and again in their walk with Christ because they don't realize that they are supposed to take control of their lives. They are plagued by all kinds of sins. That's why some people go forward at camp every year for the same thing they went forward for the years before: They don't have any self-control in their lives. They keep getting saved and asking forgiveness and asking again and again for the same thing because they have no self-control in their lives. They've begun to *think* that they can't have victory, they can't have control.

Ask God to instill in you right now a personal fervor and strength to do what's right, to control rather than be controlled by your circumstances.

Growing in Self-Control

GALATIANS 5:22–23
BUT THE FRUIT OF THE SPIRIT IS LOVE, JOY, PEACE, PATIENCE, KINDNESS,
GOODNESS, FAITHFULNESS, GENTLENESS AND SELF-CONTROL. AGAINST SUCH
THINGS THERE IS NO LAW.

2 PETER 1:5–7
FOR THIS VERY REASON, MAKE EVERY EFFORT TO ADD TO YOUR FAITH
GOODNESS; AND TO GOODNESS, KNOWLEDGE; AND TO KNOWLEDGE,
SELF-CONTROL; AND TO SELF-CONTROL, PERSEVERANCE; AND TO PERSEVERANCE,
GODLINESS; AND TO GODLINESS, BROTHERLY KINDNESS; AND TO BROTHERLY
KINDNESS, LOVE.

Take three minutes to memorize Galatians 5:22–23. When I first memorized this Scripture, I could never understand why one fruit of the Spirit was self-control. All of the other ones seemed so nice—love, kindness, and gentleness. But then self-control was thrown in there.

First of all let me explain: The fruit of the Spirit is just like the fruit on a tree. It is not something you pray for, and all of a sudden *boom,* it is there. Fruit *grows*; it doesn't miraculously appear. God wants to grow this fruit, this character of self-control, in your life. He is looking for trees in the body of Christ, men and women with fruit in their lives. And one fruit is self-control.

Being self-controlled means you are not controlled by the flesh, impulses, or emotions, but you are controlled by yourself. "Now wait a minute," you might be saying. "I want to be controlled by God, not by myself." That's the fallacy. Many people pray a prayer like this: "Lord, I give You control of my life today." And when they sin, they say, "Well, Lord, I gave You control and look what happened. It's not my fault." The problem is that they don't fully understand how God created people. He created us to be men and women who take dominion, people who take control. We are not to be controlled by things outside ourselves. We are not supposed to be controlled by drugs, alcohol, our sinful nature, foods, friends, or peer pressure. He created us to be in control. It is not bad or wrong to have self-control.

So how does the Holy Spirit play into this? When you are a sinner, you are controlled by the sinful nature; you can't help it. When you are born again, God gives you a new heart, a new nature, a new character, and He gives you *power* over your old nature. The Holy Spirit comes to live inside you. The Bible says that the same Spirit that raised Christ from the dead quickens your mortal body (Rom. 8:11). That means you didn't just get some little sweet blessing when you got saved. It means that you have the power of the living God living inside you. He has given you the power back. He has set you free from the grip of sin in your life. He has given you the power to take back charge of your life. And He wants you to grow self-control in your life.

You can see that in 2 Peter 1:5–7, God talks about adding different things to your life. He talks about adding self-control to your knowledge. As you learn more about the Word of God, more of what it means to be a Christian, start adding self-control to your knowledge. In other words, start doing what you know is right.

So it is not wrong to want to have self-control in your life—it is a fruit of the Spirit. But please understand that *you control yourself* because *He has given you the power* to control yourself. Don't blame God if you give Him control of your life and then you make mistakes. He says, "Good, you give Me control? Now I give you power to take back the areas in your life that you've been slipping up in." List some areas in which you need to build self-control in your life.

Begin praying right now, and take charge of these areas. You don't need to pray, "Lord, please help me be in control." Instead you can pray,

Lord Jesus, I take back these messed up areas of my life. I refuse to be controlled by emotion, sinful nature, peer pressure, or old habits. I thank You for the power to control my life because Your Spirit lives in me. I purpose to take control of these areas in my life and make them pleasing to You. In Jesus' name, amen.

Dead to Sin

We're talking about self-control this week and how you can get control of different areas in your life. If you're going to change this world, you're going to have to live a pure life. And to live a pure life, you're going to have to learn what it means to have self-control.

> ROMANS 6:11–14
> IN THE SAME WAY, COUNT YOURSELVES DEAD TO SIN BUT ALIVE TO GOD IN
> CHRIST JESUS. THEREFORE DO NOT LET SIN REIGN IN YOUR MORTAL BODY SO
> THAT YOU OBEY ITS EVIL DESIRES. DO NOT OFFER THE PARTS OF YOUR BODY
> TO SIN, AS INSTRUMENTS OF WICKEDNESS, BUT RATHER OFFER YOURSELVES TO
> GOD, AS THOSE WHO HAVE BEEN BROUGHT FROM DEATH TO LIFE; AND OFFER
> THE PARTS OF YOUR BODY TO HIM AS INSTRUMENTS OF RIGHTEOUSNESS. FOR
> SIN SHALL NOT BE YOUR MASTER, BECAUSE YOU ARE NOT UNDER LAW, BUT
> UNDER GRACE.

Write in your own words what you understand this passage to mean.

Paul is telling you exactly how to defeat sin in your life. He says to consider your body dead to sin. In other words, refuse to let your hands, lips, mouth, or brain be used for anything sinful. If your body is dead to sin, it cannot be used for sin. Then he says to offer the parts of your body as instruments of righteousness and not instruments of wickedness. The very fact that he tells you that you can offer your body either to righteousness or to sin tells you that you have the choice. You have the ability to be in control.

God gave you back that ability when you were born again and His Spirit came to live inside you. *It is your choice*. It is not the devil's choice. You can choose to offer your body as an instrument of sin or of righteousness. It's not your friend's choice. It's not dependent on peer pressure. It's not your parents' choice. It's your choice. You can feel guilty, or you can feel victorious.

The good news is that *the devil can't tell you what to do*. He can't force you to do anything. You are a child of God. The Bible says that you are not a slave, and the devil can't boss you around. He can't control your life anymore. The good news is that God has given you back the ability to control your destiny, to control what you do. This is the good news of the gospel.

It's not just some cheesy little thing, and one day we get to go to heaven. The good news is that right now we are not under control of the devil. Some people let sin dominate their lives because they don't know that they have a choice. They think the devil still has control over their lives because the devil has been lying to them and saying, "You can't really defeat this problem.

You can't really defeat this sin." The devil is a liar. The Bible says that it's our choice.

List some things that you have been doing that have been offering parts of your body to wickedness or sinfulness—whether they are big or small things, using your tongue in the wrong way, or whatever.

Now list some ways that you could use these parts of your body as instruments of righteousness. List things that you could do that would give God glory. Remember, it's your choice. I want to challenge you today to make the right choice. Put your foot down and say, "In Jesus' name, I refuse to let the flesh rule over me. God has given me the power and I'm going to take it."

Think of the areas that you listed as not having had control over. Put your foot down today and say, "In Jesus' name, I'm taking control of my life. I'm taking these areas back from the devil."

Be Ruthless

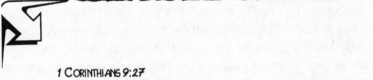

1 CORINTHIANS 9:27
I BEAT MY BODY AND MAKE IT MY SLAVE SO THAT AFTER I HAVE PREACHED TO OTHERS, I MYSELF WILL NOT BE DISQUALIFIED FOR THE PRIZE.

Rewrite this verse in your own words. What does it mean to you?

_____ ____ ____ ____ _____

_____ ____ ____ ____ _____

_____ ____ ____ ____ _____

Paul was ruthless about living a self-controlled life. I look at it like this: I don't let my body do whatever it wants to do just because it has that sinful nature living inside it. I refuse to let that sinful nature rule over me. So I beat it—I make it my slave. To beat my body means to demand that it do what I tell it to do.

And I'm telling it to line up with the Word of God. I'm telling it to do whatever is righteous, pure, and holy. Some people say, "I just can't help it. I just do that habit, that sin." I'm telling you right now, you can help it.

It's like telling your body that Daddy has come home. What do I mean by that? When you were growing up and you got in trouble, your mom might have said, "Just wait until your father gets home. Boy, you're really going to get it then!" Fear came all over you: "Wow, is he going to spank me or what?" For so long now your body has had the opportunity to do whatever it wanted to do with no self-control because you didn't control it. Now that you realize that you can control it, you have to shock your body. Wake it up and say, "Daddy has come home. You can't do whatever you used to do anymore." Say to your lips, "Lips, you don't get to say whatever you want to say. You're going to say only things that line up with the Word of God." Say to your hands, "Hands, you're not going to be used to fight people. You are going to be used to love and care for people." Say to your brain, "Brain, you are not going to think whatever you want to think. You're going to think about whatever is true, lovely, and worthy of praise."

Take four minutes right now to memorize Philippians 4:8:

WHATEVER IS TRUE, WHATEVER IS NOBLE, WHATEVER IS RIGHT, WHATEVER IS PURE, WHATEVER IS LOVELY, WHATEVER IS ADMIRABLE— IF ANYTHING IS EXCELLENT OR PRAISEWORTHY— THINK ABOUT SUCH THINGS.

When you do these things, you will find yourself developing godly habits and doing righteous things because you have self-control. You can't be jerked back and forth by impulses because you have self-control built into your life. The good news is that Jesus died to forgive you and to give you control over your destiny.

Not My Will But Yours

MARK 14:36
"ABBA, FATHER," [JESUS] SAID, "EVERYTHING IS POSSIBLE FOR YOU. TAKE THIS CUP FROM ME. YET NOT WHAT I WILL, BUT WHAT YOU WILL."

LUKE 22:42
FATHER IF YOU ARE WILLING, TAKE THIS CUP FROM ME; YET NOT MY WILL, BUT YOURS BE DONE.

Having self-control is submitting your will to God. It is saying, "Lord, my flesh or my desire would rather do something else, but I want Your desire more." Even Jesus had to deal with that. There He was in the Garden of Gethsemane waiting to be crucified. He was saying, "Lord, I'd really rather not do this. If You want Me to, I will. But if there is another plan, I'd sure like You to use it now. Not My will, but Yours be done." This should be a regular conversation between you and the Lord. When you face difficult situations, say, "Well, my flesh would rather do this. I'm really weak here. I really feel tempted here. But, Lord, I'm not going to do what my flesh wants to do or what I want to do. I'm going to do what You want me to do."

Is there something you need to do but have put off doing because you haven't wanted to do it? Write it here.

It's your choice just as it was Jesus' choice whether to go to the cross or not. God did not force Jesus to go, but Jesus submitted His will to God. He said "Lord, I don't want just what I want. I want what You want. My flesh and My heart are telling Me something else, but I'm going to purpose to do only what pleases You." Jesus was submitted to the point that He could say that the prince of this world was coming, but he had no hold on Him (John 14:30). Even though the devil is here and may be all around you, he still has no hold on you. You need to stand firm and say with conviction, "The devil can tempt me all he wants. He can blast me with all his garbage. But he has no hold on me. He has no control on my life. God gave me back control of my life when I gave Him my heart. And I choose to submit my will to God just as Jesus did."

Go back and review the Scriptures you learned this week about self-control. Begin to practice self-control in everything you do. Build this character trait into your life so that you are not an up-and-down, back-and-forth kind of person anymore. Don't keep praying weak little prayers. You have learned the truth. God has given you back control of your life. He designed you to dominate this earth and be in control of your destiny. He redeemed you, and now you have the right to use your body and your life for holy things instead of unrighteous things. Make a choice to have self-control.

WEEK 8

A Pure Heart

Challenge 6:

WorldChangers Pursue Holy Courtship
Instead of Dating

What Is a Pure Heart?

MATTHEW 5:8
BLESSED ARE THE PURE IN HEART,
FOR THEY WILL SEE GOD.

Jesus made this promise during His Sermon on the Mount. It was a commitment He was making to all who would dare to have a pure undefiled heart after God. As World-Changers, we have to be people with pure motives and pure hearts. Some people give God lip service, but they have a bunch of garbage corroding their hearts. They go to church and Christian events. Yet it seems that so much of their lives is corroded with sin. It all starts with a corroded heart. It is so much easier to live pure for the Lord when your heart is pure, when you're genuinely seeking after Him and genuinely wanting to keep every part of your life absolutely clean.

When some people give their lives to the Lord, they act as if they're following Him, but they have a hard time really connecting with Him and finding Him. Jesus makes a promise: You keep your heart pure, and you're going to see God. You're going to see Him at work in your heart. You're going to see Him at work in other people's lives. You're going to see Him at work in this world. You can see the evidence of His work all around you. It's amazing how much God can be doing all around you, but you will not see it if your heart is not pure.

You're going to have to have a pure heart to keep the sixth challenge of a WorldChanger: WorldChangers pursue holy courtship instead of dating. It's not enough just to have a pure body; you've got to have a pure heart. The commitment to stay pure and only court until you're married doesn't start with the commitment not to have sex; it starts with the commitment to have a pure heart.

 Take some time right now to think about things you may have in your heart that have been corrupting your heart or your walk with God in any way. Maybe they corrupt the way you look at people or your perspective on life. List these things here.

———— ————————— —————— ————————

———— ————————— ————————— ————

———— ————————— ————————— ————

Ask God to forgive you right now. Meditate on Matthew 5:8 all day today. Chew on it and claim the promise. Pray with freedom,

> *Lord, I've got a pure heart. I've given everything to You, so now I want to see You today in my heart and in my life. In Jesus' name, amen.*

A Clean Heart

PSALM 24:3-4
WHO MAY ASCEND THE HILL OF THE LORD?
WHO MAY STAND IN HIS HOLY PLACE?
HE WHO HAS CLEAN HANDS AND A PURE HEART,
WHO DOES NOT LIFT UP HIS SOUL TO AN IDOL
OR SWEAR BY WHAT IS FALSE.

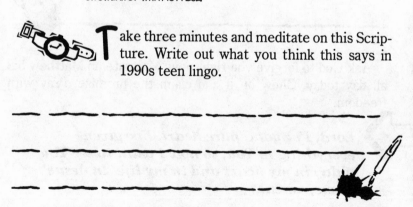

Take three minutes and meditate on this Scripture. Write out what you think this says in 1990s teen lingo.

The psalmist, David, is asking who God will accept on His holy hill. In other words, who will God let get tight with Him?

Who will God allow to grab hold of Him? To whom will He reveal the secrets of His heart? David answers the question: "Those who have clean hands and a pure heart." If what you do with your hands is clean and pure and if what's going on inside your heart is clean and pure, you can stand with Him.

God is looking for a new generation of young people with clean hands and pure hearts. He is looking for young people who will constantly go to the mountain of the Lord, who will constantly go back to hang out with Him and get tight with Him. He is looking for people who are constantly thinking not just about what they do but about what's going on in their hearts. Is it clean? Is it acceptable before God? Is it pure?

Jesus washed your heart with forgiveness when you first gave your life to Him. He cleansed your heart of all impurities. Now it's so important to make sure that you receive His cleansing and forgiveness every day, that you do everything with a pure motive and a pure perspective. Make sure everything you do is motivated by a heart that longs after Him.

God allows only one kind of person to get tight with Him, only one kind of person to hang out with Him. Only one kind of person could, as Moses did, go up and be on the top of the mountain to hang out with God. Only those with pure lives and pure hearts get to really connect with God. Today, make it your aim to have *a pure heart all day long*. Think only of things that would glorify Him.

Hearing from God

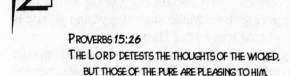

PROVERBS 15:26
THE LORD DETESTS THE THOUGHTS OF THE WICKED,
BUT THOSE OF THE PURE ARE PLEASING TO HIM.

We're talking about having a pure heart. We're talking about being someone who is characterized by always having pure motives and a pure heart. We've discussed several advantages of having a pure heart. Can you list some of them here?

When you have a pure heart, even your thoughts please God. Here's a glimpse of what happens when you have a pure heart. When you keep your mind, your heart, and your motives totally clean and bathed in the blood of Jesus, asking forgiveness, focusing your energies on only doing what is pure and right, you begin to get a Holy Spirit–anointed thought life. Your mind will be cleared up enough so that you can hear things from God that you have never heard before. God is so pleased when you have a pure heart and begin to think pure thoughts so that His Spirit finds it easy to be at home in your thought life. Then you can start hearing things from God's Spirit that you never heard before because you have cleaned out the pipes enough to allow His words to flow into you.

What an incredible advantage it is to have a pure heart! You'll hear things from God that many people never get to hear. You'll be way different from the "average Joe" youth group member who just goes to youth group but then tries to get away with everything he can through the rest of the week. You have the ability to tap into the holy God who created this whole universe.

I want you to take Proverbs 15:26 with you all day long. Memorize it and meditate on it. Write it on an index card and carry it with you all day long. Keep your mind on this Scripture, and keep your heart pure all day. When thoughts come to your mind that you think are from God but you are not really sure, write them down. You'll be amazed at how many things you'll begin to pick up: that God is speaking to you, wanting you to do things, giving you wisdom on how to do things, giving you wisdom on how to interact in relationships at school, how to witness, how to do better at your job so you'll get a promotion, how to get better grades. He'll give you supernatural remembrance of things for your tests. But it all starts with a pure heart. Try it today and see how it goes!

Purity in Your Thoughts

2 TIMOTHY 2:22
FLEE THE EVIL DESIRES OF YOUTH, AND PURSUE RIGHTEOUSNESS, FAITH, LOVE
AND PEACE, ALONG WITH THOSE WHO CALL ON THE LORD OUT OF A PURE
HEART.

1 TIMOTHY 5:2
[TREAT] OLDER WOMEN AS MOTHERS, YOUNGER WOMEN AS SISTERS, WITH ALL
PURITY (NKJV).

W hat do these two verses mean to you, personally,
today?

_____

_____

_____

Take five minutes to memorize both of these Scriptures right now. Paul is dealing with probably one of the biggest struggles young people have. As you begin to develop physically, it is only normal for you to notice people of the opposite sex. The Bible is clear on this subject. Impure thoughts are called lust. In a depraved world it is normal to have lustful thoughts. But you, as a man or woman of God, need to get smart and guard yourself. Run from these things and keep your heart pure.

We're talking about having a pure heart this week. It can't be just a lot of nice flowery words. It's got to come down to gut-level honesty. Many guys look at girls and have lustful thoughts. Many young ladies think sensually about guys they might like.

You need to wash your mind of this garbage. Start looking people in the eyes rather than up and down their bodies to see what they look like. Start caring about them as people. Start looking at them as valuable human beings who have a lot to offer this world. They may be really hurting, busted, and broken. They may have been treated in an impure way their whole lives. If you look at them in an impure way, you add to the problem rather than protect them from it.

The Bible says, "To the pure, all things are pure" (Titus 1:15). In other words, if your heart is pure—genuinely pure, genuinely forgiven, and thinking on the things of God—then when you look at people of the opposite sex, the first thing that will pop into your mind will be something positive, holy, and pure. It's time for a new generation of young people to commit to having a pure heart in the way they look at people of the opposite sex.

Today, I want you to practice this. As you go to school or work, practice looking at people in their eyes. As you look at them in the eyes, just imagine: If you were Jesus, how would you be looking at them? What would you be thinking about them while you're talking to them? Take these two Scriptures in 1 and 2 Timothy with you. Write them down. Meditate on them all day long. As you interact with people today, practice having a pure heart in the way you see them.

Forgiven

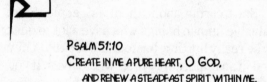

PSALM 51:10
CREATE IN ME A PURE HEART, O GOD,
AND RENEW A STEADFAST SPIRIT WITHIN ME.

Rewrite this verse in 1990s teen language.

_____

_____

_____

Take three minutes right now to meditate on this verse. David prayed this prayer after he had really blown it with Bathsheba. You can read about this situation in 2 Samuel 11—12. David had committed adultery with another man's wife and gotten her pregnant. Then he sent that man to his death so he could marry the man's wife. Later, when he realized he had sinned, he came running back to God and cried out for God to create a pure heart within him.

Maybe you have been impure in the past in a relationship with someone of the opposite sex. It's time for you to pray the same prayer that David prayed. Say,

> **God, create in me a clean heart. Lord, I don't want to be harassed for the rest of my life by the impure things I've done in my past. In Jesus' name, amen.**

You don't need to be harassed. Many times people who previously have been sexually involved replay like a videotape in their minds the thing that happened. They watch it over and over and over again. They fight the battle in their minds because of what they are thinking about all the time.

I want to encourage you that if you have been sexually involved or into any kind of impurity, anytime you think of the memories: (1) ask God to forgive you and to cleanse your heart; (2) forgive yourself and forgive the other person for taking advantage of the moment (sometimes the harder thing to do is to forgive yourself for violating your own conscience); and (3) take some time to pray for that person. Instead of just thinking about the things you did together, look at that person the way Jesus would. Pray for him that God will change his life and draw him closer to Himself. Or pray for her, as an individual, that she will come to find who Jesus really is and get her life radically changed.

MISSIONS IS...
having to totally
rely on God.
—Joy

Let me also say this to you: Maybe you haven't

messed up physically, but you have messed up a lot mentally. Many people pride themselves on the fact that they are virgins physically, but in their minds they are not virgins at all. If this describes you, you need to repent just as much as those who have actually committed the physical act.

David cried out for a pure heart. We are talking about it all week long. You need to be a virgin in your heart and in your mind as well as in your body. You cannot stand pridefully looking down at somebody who has messed up physically if in your heart you lust or you think about other people in an impure way. God wants you to be a virgin with a pure heart as well as a pure body.

Make David's prayer your prayer. Say,

> *God, create in me a clean heart regarding the way I look at people. Create in me a clean heart for the way I have been involved with people in the past.*

Take some time right now and pray over the people you have been involved with in the past or you have thought about in an impure way. When you leave your quiet time, your heart and mind can be pure toward these people, and you will have forgiven yourself once and for all.

The Motives of Your Heart

1 CORINTHIANS 4:5

JUDGE NOTHING BEFORE THE APPOINTED TIME; WAIT TILL THE LORD COMES. HE WILL BRING TO LIGHT WHAT IS HIDDEN IN DARKNESS AND WILL EXPOSE THE MOTIVES OF MEN'S HEARTS. AT THAT TIME EACH WILL RECEIVE HIS PRAISE FROM GOD.

1 CHRONICLES 28:9

AND YOU, MY SON SOLOMON, ACKNOWLEDGE THE GOD OF YOUR FATHER, AND SERVE HIM WITH WHOLEHEARTED DEVOTION AND WITH A WILLING MIND, FOR THE LORD SEARCHES EVERY HEART AND UNDERSTANDS EVERY MOTIVE BEHIND THE THOUGHTS. IF YOU SEEK HIM, HE WILL BE FOUND BY YOU; BUT IF YOU FORSAKE HIM, HE WILL REJECT YOU FOREVER.

Having a pure heart has to do with motives. It doesn't just have to do with having pure relationships with people of the opposite sex. It has to do with being pure in the way you look at life, relationships, and business dealings; the way you treat your boss; and the way you do your homework. Having a pure heart means treating people with purity the way Jesus would treat them. God weighs motives. He doesn't just

MISSIONS IS...
giving people a
chance at real life.
—Candace

care about what you do; He cares about the motives of your heart. He wants your motives to be pure. He measures the motives; He knows what they are. That's God's agenda.

Your goal in life in pleasing the Lord is not just to do pleasing things but to do pleasing things with the right motive—a motive that's generated out of a pure love for God and a desire to do what's right. You may do "right things" sometimes because you think you will get noticed or because it's the right thing to do when someone is looking at you. But you can tell if your motives are pure when even though no one will notice, you are still committed and determined to do what is right.

Somebody might want to be the captain of the basketball team because it fills something in her ego. A person might want to be a boss because he likes to tell people what to do. Neither person has a pure heart or considers that it might be better for the team if someone else is the captain or for the job if someone else is in charge. People with an impure heart always want their way. In any kind of relationship with friends they don't think about God's best in the situation or have pure motives.

I want you to list some things that you've done or thought in your relationships with your friends that have come out of impure motives.

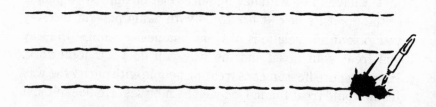

How can you correct these things?

_____

_____

_____

Now ask God to forgive you and ask Him for His mind, for His heart so that you launch into life in every area with a pure heart after God and with pure motives in everything you set your hand to do.

Week 8

DAY 7

Set Your Mind on Pure Things

1 TIMOTHY 1:5
THE GOAL OF THIS COMMAND IS LOVE, WHICH COMES FROM A PURE HEART AND A GOOD CONSCIENCE AND A SINCERE FAITH.

PHILIPPIANS 4:8
WHATEVER IS TRUE, WHATEVER IS NOBLE, WHATEVER IS RIGHT, WHATEVER IS PURE, WHATEVER IS LOVELY, WHATEVER IS ADMIRABLE—IF ANYTHING IS EXCELLENT OR PRAISEWORTHY—THINK ABOUT SUCH THINGS.

Take five minutes right now to think about what these Scriptures really mean. Think about the main point of each Scripture. Write down what you think is the main point of each Scripture.

1 Timothy 1:5: ______________________________

____

____

Philippians 4:8: ___ ___ ___ ___ ___ ___ ___ ___

___ ___ ___ ___ ___ ___ ___

___ ___ ___ ___ ___

This week we are talking about having a pure heart in everything. The first verse says that love coming from a pure heart is what this whole Christian life is about. We must love our neighbors, our enemies, people at school and work, and people of the opposite sex. God wants us to have a love that comes from a pure heart.

The second verse gives us a clear picture of how to keep the mind and the heart pure: by keeping the mind dwelling on things that are awesome, excellent, and praiseworthy, things that will give glory to God. I know that you, as a young person, might think, *How in the world can I keep these things in my mind when I am bombarded with so many bad things all day long?* Well, you have to set your mind on the things above (Col. 3:2). You have to choose to set your mind on pure things. Having a pure heart means your heart has been refined.

When gold or silver is refined, it is heated to extremely high temperatures, which causes the impurities to rise to the top. The refiners can then scoop off the impurities. God wants to do the same thing in your heart today and every day. He wants to heat up your heart. Fuse it with His Word as you keep your mind on whatever is pure. As the impurities come to the top, you repent. Then God scrapes the impurities off, and your whole life becomes a little more pure. Then tomorrow He heats up your heart a little more, and more impurities come to the top. When you repent, He scrapes these impurities off, too. Each day you get purer and purer. Your motives, relationships, and attitudes are constantly being refined and made more pure.

Having a pure heart is a character trait that is to be valued

MISSIONS HAS
GIVEN ME...
a deeper walk with God.
—Lauri

above anything because, as Jesus promised in Matthew 5, those who have a pure heart will see God. The psalms tell us that people with a pure heart will hang out on His holy hill and hear His voice as He speaks to them in their thoughts. When you seek a pure heart with everything in you, you separate yourself from "average Joe" Christians in this world who are content with looking the Christian part on the outside but have corrupt hearts. You have to have a pure heart to keep your relationship with God right. You have to have a pure heart to pursue a courtship that is holy and to keep a godly romance pure. A pure romance doesn't begin after you get in the romance. It comes by practicing to have a pure heart right now in everything you say and do.

Review your memory verses from this week. Chew on them all day long. Practice fleeing youthful lusts today. Practice keeping your mind set on whatever is pure today. Practice looking at people with a pure heart and with pure motives right into their eyes, and watch how God will begin to revolutionize your life and you'll walk closer and closer to the top of that holy hill and hang out at the top, just as Moses did.

WEEK 9

Humility

Challenge 7:
WorldChangers Honor Their Parents

Cast Your Cares on Him

JAMES 4:10
HUMBLE YOURSELVES BEFORE THE LORD, AND HE WILL LIFT YOU UP.

1 PETER 5:6 – 7
HUMBLE YOURSELVES, THEREFORE, UNDER GOD'S MIGHTY HAND, THAT HE MAY LIFT YOU UP IN DUE TIME. CAST ALL YOUR ANXIETY ON HIM BECAUSE HE CARES FOR YOU.

This week we will talk about humility. God is looking for young men and women who will be genuinely humble. He doesn't want a fake humility that says, "I'm really a nothing," but inside is conceited and arrogant. You know, some people think that humility is saying or feeling that they are a nothing. Really the very opposite is true. God says you can do all things through Christ (Phil. 4:13). He says you're the apple of His eye (Zech. 2:8). He says you're beautifully and wonderfully made (Ps. 139:14). You're not a nothing. True humility is knowing and recognizing who God is and recognizing who you are. He is God, and you're a human being. He is the most incredible Being in the universe, and you're the apple of His eye.

James 4:10 and 1 Peter 5:6–7 are probably the most famous of all humility Scriptures. Some people think these Scriptures say, "Humble yourself in the sight of the Lord, and He will stomp your head." In reality God says, "Humble yourself and keep yourself in right relationship with Me, recognizing that I'm the Lord and you're My servant, and I will *lift you up*."

First Peter 5:6–7 says that to stay humble, you need to cast all your cares on God. When things are bothering or harassing you, or when the devil is trying to mess up your head, cast it all on Him because He cares for you. By giving all your worries to God and laying them at His feet, you're saying, "Lord, I can't do this without You; I need Your help in these areas." Then you leave the cares at His feet. You humble yourself before Him.

List some cares or troubles that you have been trying to handle on your own.

Now cast them at His feet. Just give them over to Him. Pray this prayer:

> *Lord, I commit to humble myself before You, and I continue to recognize that You are the Son of God and You have saved me. In Jesus' name, amen.*

I want you to take these Scriptures with you and meditate on them all day long. Continually humble yourself in the sight of the Lord, and feel the strength of God lifting you up as you constantly humble yourself before Him all day today.

The Power of Humility

MATTHEW 11:28-30

COME TO ME, ALL YOU WHO ARE WEARY AND BURDENED, AND I WILL GIVE YOU REST. TAKE MY YOKE UPON YOU AND LEARN FROM ME, FOR I AM GENTLE AND HUMBLE IN HEART, AND YOU WILL FIND REST FOR YOUR SOULS. FOR MY YOKE IS EASY AND MY BURDEN IS LIGHT.

Take three minutes to meditate on these verses.

Jesus said, "If you feel weak or burdened, come to Me. Take My yoke upon you." Then He described a little bit of His character. He said, "I am gentle and humble in heart." Now, some people think, *Man, Jesus must be a wimp—He is gentle and humble.* Jesus came as the most powerful human being ever to walk on this earth. Yet, at the same time, He was the most humble. He didn't have to prove anything to anybody. He *knew* He was the Son of God, so He didn't have to walk around in arrogance trying to prove everything.

Jesus came in humility. He walked as a human being and

wasn't trying to show off all the time. He had a humble attitude. He said, "I am gentle and humble in heart." Don't mistake this for thinking Jesus was a wimp. Remember when Jesus went to the temple and saw all the money changers and unrighteous people there? He threw everybody out of the temple. He thundered as He preached to the Pharisees and the Sadducees about their hypocrisy. He wasn't a wimp; He was strong. He knew who He was, but at the same time, He looked people in the eyes and He cared for them. He wasn't puffed up and trying to put Himself above them all the time. In fact, He washed the disciples' feet. He said, "I came to serve you." The kind of strength Jesus showed us is the kind of strength that comes through being humble and serving other people.

MISSIONS IS...
God's love being
represented through those
who realize their love
is not enough.
—Danielle

We're talking about humility this week, and the challenge that correlates with this is honoring your parents. Too many people in this world think it's a weak thing to honor your parents. They make you feel that you must not be very strong if you have to submit to them and do everything they say. But Jesus has a different measure of strength. He measures strength by how humble you are. The more humble you are, the stronger you are. You're not being sucked into a peer pressure ideal that shows a *false sense of strength* by getting to do whatever you want. You show that you're strong by humbling yourself and serving other people.

If you are carrying any burdens or worries that you need to give over to God, write them out here. As you write, imagine yourself laying each of them at God's feet and humbly accepting His rest for you.

I want you to take Matthew 11:28–30 and meditate on it. Get it down in your spirit today. Take it with you all day long. Every time you see the ugly face of arrogance trying to get into your life, chew on this Scripture: "I am gentle and humble in heart; I am gentle and humble in heart." Say it about yourself until it becomes second nature to you. You don't have to go out and prove anything to anybody today. You are a daughter or son of God. God knows it and you know it. Now go out and act like it. Be humble about it in everything you do and every attitude you reflect.

Serving Others

W e're talking about being humble and gentle again today. You can really tell if people are humble and gentle by the degree that they are willing to bear with others. Do they listen to others and serve them as Jesus did? Arrogant people don't have time to meet others' needs. They don't have time to listen to people. They think they are too important to slow down and care.

Being humble is not acting like a worm. Being humble is knowing that, in Christ, you are a strong man or woman. It doesn't intimidate you to slow down and listen to, or spend time with, even people who aren't popular. Some people don't want to be seen with people who aren't popular. They don't want to bear with others because they're afraid of what it will do for their reputation or of what other people will think of them. Jesus never cared what people thought of Him.

The Bible commands us to be completely humble. Don't just

try to be humble; *make a decision to be humble*. It's really easy to be humble if you continually see yourself as a servant. We're not here to be in charge of people or to tell them what to do. We're here to serve them.

Make a list of some people you can serve today as you go to school or to work.

Now make a decision to walk into this day with a servant's attitude ready to bend over backward serving the people you listed. Serve your parents so you can live the challenge of honoring them today.

MISSIONS HAS GIVEN ME...
a greater compassion for the people of the world.
—Ashley

Meek or Weak?

NUMBERS 12:3
NOW THE MAN MOSES WAS VERY MEEK, ABOVE ALL THE MEN WHICH WERE UPON
THE FACE OF THE EARTH (KJV).

W hat do you think it means that Moses was the meekest man on earth?

Moses was just back from getting in Pharaoh's face. All the plagues had come—the flies, the hail, the river turned to blood, the deaths of the firstborn—and he had led tons of people out of Egypt. He had parted the Red Sea and walked through it with all the children of Israel. Then it had closed over the whole army of

Egypt. Next, Moses walked up the mountain where he met face-to-face with God and received the Ten Commandments written on stone tablets by the hand of God. When Moses walked back down into camp, his face was glowing. Yet, after all that, the Bible says he was the meekest man on earth.

Please do not misinterpret the word *meek* to mean "weak." Some people think that being humble or meek is a sign of weakness, that being gentle is a sign of weakness. Men especially have a tendency to think this way. However, *meekness* means "controlled power." Think about it. Someone knows he has power, he knows he is strong, but he controls it. He chooses to be humble instead of flaunting it or bragging about it all the time. The Bible says that Moses was the meekest man on earth. He knew the power he had; he knew that the words he spoke were the words of the living God and that his actions set a whole nation free. He parted an entire sea, and he spoke to God face-to-face. Yet his attitude was meek and humble.

God is looking for people today who have controlled power. That is meekness: people who know who they are, who know the strength they have in God, and who refuse to back down. Yet when you look in the faces of these people, you will see humility and gentleness. These people know it's going to take a servant's attitude to reach other people. When it comes to the devil, these people know they have the strength in the name of Jesus to kick in the devil's face. But when it comes to other people, they are meek and humble.

It's almost as though it is a paradox: You know you are strong, but you don't brag about it. You only brag about it to the devil when you're in your quiet time so you can put him in his place. Stand up today and walk off with a servant's attitude.

You'll Be Blessed

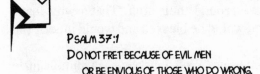

PSALM 37:1
DO NOT FRET BECAUSE OF EVIL MEN
 OR BE ENVIOUS OF THOSE WHO DO WRONG.

MATTHEW 5:5
BLESSED ARE THE MEEK,
 FOR THEY WILL INHERIT THE EARTH.

Rewrite these verses in your own words.

_____

_____

_____
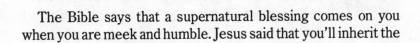

The Bible says that a supernatural blessing comes on you when you are meek and humble. Jesus said that you'll inherit the earth. What does that mean? It means that you will be in charge and in control of the things on this earth. You will have a chance to inherit, or be in charge of, worldly things because God can trust you with them.

Too many people in America live way beyond their means. They drive a nice car; they have a big house, a big boat, and a big ego. But they have to rob Peter to pay Paul because they're extended beyond their level of income. God is looking to definitely bless His people. The kind of people He can bless the most are people who are meek, people who have controlled power, people who are humble, people who know they are strong in the Lord.

The people God can trust the most with money are ones who are humble in heart because they know that their egos and attitudes do not revolve around their stuff. That's why Jesus promised that the meek would be blessed and would inherit the things on this earth.

We may hear someone say, "Well, I just live in a humble little house." So we think that if we're going to be humble, we have to be poor and have nothing. Actually, according to this Scripture, the very opposite is true. When you show God that you're going to have a humble heart, He will bless your face off.

Right now is the time to take this Scripture, chew on it all day long, and let the prayer of your heart be this:

Oh, God, please let me be one of the meek, humble men and women of God You can trust with the things of this earth so I can use the things of this earth to glorify You. In Jesus' name, amen.

 Take a few minutes now to meditate on Psalm 37:1 and Matthew 5:5. Memorize these two Scriptures and continue to chew on them as you think about humility today.

Week 9 DAY 6

Grace to the Humble

JAMES 4:6
GOD RESISTS THE PROUD, BUT GIVES GRACE TO THE HUMBLE (NKJV).

1 PETER 5:5
YOUNG MEN, IN THE SAME WAY BE SUBMISSIVE TO THOSE WHO ARE OLDER. ALL
OF YOU, CLOTHE YOURSELVES WITH HUMILITY TOWARD ONE ANOTHER, BECAUSE,
"GOD OPPOSES THE PROUD
BUT GIVES GRACE TO THE HUMBLE."

The Bible shows us once again God's attitude toward people who are proud: He opposes them. I think the truth is, there are a lot of proud Christians who are prideful because of what they own or do for a living. As a result, God opposes them. If there's one thing you don't want, it's God opposing you because whatever God opposes will fall. But He gives grace, or power, to the humble. Another word for grace is *power*.

You are commanded in 1 Peter 5:5 to clothe yourself with humility. That means you have to put it on. It may not be the natural thing for you to be humble, but you've got to put on humility on a regular basis. You have to make a deliberate choice to have an attitude of servanthood, to bend over backward to serve people. Others should see an attitude in you that says, "You are important to me, and you are important to God." How are you going to let people in this world know that they are important to God unless you show them that they are important to you?

Too many people walk through life with a big ego, acting as if everything's cool when everything's not cool at all. And the reason life is not cool for them is that God opposes them.

It is not possible for things to be cool if God goes against you. Are there things in your life that are not coming from a humble heart? Are there areas of your life where God is opposing you because you have had an ungodly pride? Write these things here.

I want you to take 1 Peter 5:5 and continue to renew your mind about being a woman or man of humility. Pray it about yourself today. Say,

Lord, I choose to put on humility today. I choose to put on a humble attitude today even though it doesn't come naturally. I'm going to be humble by finding ways that I can serve people today. In Jesus' name, amen.

Be sure to deal specifically today with the areas you just wrote about.

Honor Your Parents

PROVERBS 15:1
A GENTLE ANSWER TURNS AWAY WRATH,
BUT A HARSH WORD STIRS UP ANGER.

W hat do you think this verse means in 1990s teenage language?

_____

_____

_____

Having a gentle answer is just one example of being humble in the midst of a tense situation. God wants us to be people of humility. Humility should spread to all areas of our lives. It should spread into our friendships, into the relationship between our youth pastor and pastor and us and, of course, into the relationship with our parents.

The challenge this week is honoring your parents, and as you maintain a humble attitude in everything that you do, it's going to be easy for you to honor your parents. There are many times when you may be tempted to smart off to your parents and say something that you know will really rip on them, something that you know will get to their hearts, especially when you know they are wrong. But you've got to be radically committed to humility in every area, not weakness in every area, but controlled power.

You need to have a servant's attitude, even though you know who you are in Christ. You know that you are a strong child of God. You belong to the most high God, and the power of the Holy Spirit lives inside you. Yet you choose to be a servant. In the same way, Jesus knew He was the Son of God, and He could command ten thousand angels to help Him at any moment, yet He chose to give up His life to die on a cross. God is so insistent on having a humble attitude toward parents that in the Old Testament, He actually commanded them to stone people who didn't respect their parents (Lev. 20:9).

God wants young people who know how to respect and act humbly toward authority. You might need to go to your parents to ask them to forgive you for arrogance that you've had toward them. Right now is the time to turn over a new leaf and make a commitment to have the character trait of humility in your life. Choose to clothe yourself with humility in all areas. In situations where you could cause a fight or be tempted to prove that you are right, choose a gentle answer and turn away wrath instead of inciting other people to jump into a conflict. Then when people look at you, they'll say, "I know that she is strong in the Lord. Yet she is so humble, it seems that every time I'm around her, all she wants to do is serve or do something to pour her life out for other people." In that, you reflect the life of the Lord and will draw more people to Him.

WEEK 10

Hard
Work

Challenge 8:
WorldChangers Are Committed to Their Church and Their Youth Group

God Is Not Afraid to Work

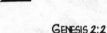

GENESIS 2:2

BY THE SEVENTH DAY GOD HAD FINISHED THE WORK HE HAD BEEN DOING; SO ON THE SEVENTH DAY HE RESTED FROM ALL HIS WORK.

et me put it plainly. To change the world, you're going to have to know how to work hard. You're going to have to get used to letting your sweat count for the kingdom of God. Many young people don't like the word *work*. They think God just wants to hassle them and busy up their lives with a bunch of things that look "churchy." Let's face it, when there is work to be done at church, most young people are not bending over backward trying to be the first ones to volunteer to get the work done.

Here in Genesis we see a different perspective on work. God worked when He created the world. The definition for the word *work* indicates that He was involved with His business, industrious, occupied, involved in a ministry. Ministry is equated with work. God was working when He was putting the world together. He said, "Let there be light." He spoke everything into being. He was working; He was creating; He was doing something. When He created human beings on the sixth day, He took His own hand and formed them.

God is not afraid to work. If you look around the world, you'll see the evidence of His work everywhere. God created us to be workers as well. And as a result of our work, awesome things can happen.

Some people just toil under the heavy load of work, dragging themselves through it, dreading every day of it. That's because they're not working the way God designed for people to work. They're just working for a paycheck, and they can't wait until their vacation.

MISSIONS IS...
hearts being made
whole by God.
—Russell

But God is a working God. According to Genesis 2:15, He put Adam in the Garden and told him to work the Garden and to take care of it. God worked to make the world. Then He wanted Adam to work to take care of it. God made it awesome; He wanted Adam to maintain it. He wanted Adam to let his energy count for something incredible.

God needs some young people who aren't afraid to work or to sweat. He wants people to look at this generation and see young people who are using their energy for things that matter, using their sweat to do something for the kingdom of God. They're not just trying to earn more money at a fast-food place so that they can buy more pizzas for themselves. They're using their energy for something that will count for eternity.

Have you been opposed to work? Do you moan anytime you're asked to take out the garbage or do something around the house? It's time to start changing that attitude right now. List some things that you know you should do but that you have complained about.

It's time to start saying,

> *Lord, teach me how to work hard like You did.*
> *Teach me how to do the kind of work that You*
> *wanted Adam to do so that my work isn't a*
> *burden. I know now that work is not a heavy*
> *weight. It's a joy, and it counts for eternity. In*
> *Jesus' name, amen.*

Look for opportunities today to serve, to work, to lighten a load for somebody else.

Work for the Kingdom

Read Matthew 20:1–16 in your Bible.

Jesus was sharing a parable about a man who was hiring people to work in his vineyard. He was equating it with His Father in heaven enlisting people to work in His vineyard. He drew several conclusions. One was that no matter when you come to work in His vineyard, you're still going to get paid the same—eternal life. But the other point was that when you give your heart to the Lord, He expects you to go to work in His vineyard. In other words, He expects you to use your energy and sweat to do something that will produce a healthy crop for Him. He is not expecting you to just give your life to the Lord and lie around in church all your life until you die and go to heaven. He is looking for people who want to use their sweat to change this world.

In Matthew 21:28–31, Jesus told another parable:

"WHAT DO YOU THINK? THERE WAS A MAN WHO HAD TWO SONS. HE WENT TO THE FIRST AND SAID, 'SON, GO AND WORK TODAY IN THE VINEYARD.' 'I WILL NOT,' HE ANSWERED, BUT LATER HE CHANGED HIS MIND AND WENT. THEN THE

FATHER WENT TO THE OTHER SON AND SAID THE SAME THING. HE ANSWERED, 'I WILL, SIR,' BUT HE DID NOT GO. WHICH OF THE TWO DID WHAT HIS FATHER WANTED?" "THE FIRST," THEY ANSWERED. JESUS SAID TO THEM, "I TELL YOU THE TRUTH, THE TAX COLLECTORS AND THE PROSTITUTES ARE ENTERING THE KINGDOM OF GOD AHEAD OF YOU. FOR JOHN CAME TO YOU TO SHOW YOU THE WAY OF RIGHTEOUSNESS, AND YOU DID NOT BELIEVE HIM, BUT THE TAX COLLECTORS AND THE PROSTITUTES DID. AND EVEN AFTER YOU SAW THIS, YOU DID NOT REPENT AND BELIEVE HIM."

Jesus was talking about two specific people who were asked to get busy and start working for the kingdom of God. One said, "Yes," but decided not to do it. The other said, "No," but then changed his mind and said, "Yeah, I'm going to go for it." Let me make this clear: We definitely do not work for our salvation—it is a free gift from God. He gave us forgiveness and grace. We come to Him with a pure heart, with a passion for Him, to love Him with all our hearts. Once we're in the kingdom, what He has done in us is so real that we want to use our energy to work the vineyard and to spread the gospel with all that passion.

This week we're talking about becoming a hard worker. You're going to need this quality to keep challenge 8: WorldChangers are committed to their church and their youth group. Your youth pastor and your pastor need you to work hard. They need young men and women of God who have a regular habit of working hard. They need people who love to work hard for the kingdom of God because they know it will count for something. They need people who'd rather work hard for a youth group activity than at football or cheerleading practice because they know the work for the youth ministry will reap eternal fruit and results.

What are some things you know your pastor and

MISSIONS HAS GIVEN ME...
discipline.
—Eugene

youth pastor would appreciate your doing to help them? List them here.

_____

_____

_____

Ask the Lord today,

Lord, what work do You have for me in Your vineyard? What part of the vineyard can I work in? Lord, I want to use my sweat, I want to use my energy, to do something that counts, something that matters for eternity. In Jesus' name, amen.

Then look for opportunities to serve. Ask your youth pastor and your pastor today, "What can I do for you? How can I use my energy to help with your vision to expand the kingdom of God?"

Week 10

DAY 3

Working for the Lord

COLOSSIANS 3:22-23

SLAVES, OBEY YOUR EARTHLY MASTERS IN EVERYTHING; AND DO IT, NOT ONLY WHEN THEIR EYE IS ON YOU AND TO WIN THEIR FAVOR, BUT WITH SINCERITY OF HEART AND REVERENCE FOR THE LORD. WHATEVER YOU DO, WORK AT IT WITH ALL YOUR HEART, AS WORKING FOR THE LORD, NOT FOR MEN.

T ake three minutes to meditate on and memorize these verses. It has been said of this generation of teenagers that they are lazy. They are slackers. They don't really want to work hard and don't really care about their jobs or what they're doing. Although it is true that many young people have been raised under the auspices of movies and TV, and so it would be very easy to want to be a slug when all you've been is a couch potato your whole life, I don't think that is the real problem. I think the real problem is that young people haven't found anything that is worth working their hearts out for. They think, *So what? Why should I work hard for money? My parents give me money. And so what if I did work hard for money? It wouldn't really bring me happiness because my parents have worked hard for money and we have lots of it, but we're not really that happy.*

The problem isn't necessarily having a desire to work or not. The problem is finding something that is worth working your heart out for. In this passage Paul encourages the slaves to work hard for their masters as they would work for the Lord. He is talking about establishing a work ethic; no matter what you do, you work hard as if Jesus were your boss. If you think you're just doing what your mom and dad, youth group, youth pastor, or pastor tells you to do, then it's not very motivating. But if you realize that Jesus is your boss and He establishes authority, then when your authority figures ask you to do something, it's as if the Lord is asking you to do something. And when you obey, you should do it with all your heart, even when no one is looking, because you want to please the Lord. Know that the Lord sees your work and will be pleased with what you do.

In 1 Corinthians 15:58, Paul says, "Therefore, my dear brothers, stand firm. Let nothing move you. Always give yourselves fully to the work of the Lord, because you know that your labor in the Lord is not in vain." When Paul talks about giving yourself fully to the work of the Lord, he is saying, "Here is one thing that you could pour everything out for." He is identifying the thing that so many young people are looking for—something that is worth putting their strength into, something that is worth sinking their teeth into. This is it! It's the work of the kingdom of God! It'll change the world forever and ever. It'll mean people end up in heaven rather than hell. That's worth doing whatever you have to do to make it happen. Paul is exhorting the people in Corinth, saying, "This is the kind of people I want you to be. I want you to be the kind who pour your guts out to change this world. I want you to be the kind of people who are not afraid to sweat, not afraid to work hard, not afraid to do whatever it takes because people's lives are at stake."

Remember, we're not trying to earn anything with this work we're doing. We're just so amazed that God has changed our lives, it is an honor that He could use our sweat to help make something of eternal good. Ask the Lord today,

Lord, what could I do? How could I use some of my sweat and energy today to expand Your kingdom?

Write down any ideas you get.

_____ _____ _____ _____ _____ _____

_____ _____ _____ _____ _____

_____ _____ _____ _____ _____

I want to challenge you today to change your schedule. Make time to talk to your pastor or youth pastor, your parents—somebody—today, and ask, "Is there anything that I can do today to use some of my energy for the kingdom of God? I don't want to just live through another day using my energy for things in this world that aren't even worthwhile. I want to make some of my energy today count for eternity." This is one reason mission trips are so great! They give young people an opportunity to use their energy to change the world.

Use Your Energy for God

Turn to Mark 6:30–46 in your Bible and read it. Once you've read it, take a few minutes and list some of the physical work the disciples did on this day.

As you can see, this is an average day in the lives of the disciples. They didn't just hang out with Jesus and listen to parables and watch the miracles; they were actually doing work with Jesus. He was the One multiplying the fish and the bread in the story, but they were also directly connected to the miracles through their work. They were distributing the miracle. They were making it possible for others to experience the miracle. It wasn't just a dream day of a lot of fun for them to carry baskets back and forth all afternoon. First, they had to make all of the people sit down in groups of fifty, more than five thousand of them. Next, they had to take the food out basket by basket and feed them all. Then, they had to take all the leftovers and put them back in the baskets. Finally, they had to get into the boat and row across the lake. All in one day. I imagine it could have been really easy for some of those guys to have bad attitudes about it, saying, "Come on, Jesus. I didn't sign up for this. I just want to be a disciple. I just want to hang around and listen to You."

Many young people at church are saying the same stuff: "I didn't sign up for this. I just want to come to youth group. I just want to come to all the activities. I don't want to do anything." But God is looking for some young people who aren't afraid to sweat as the disciples did. He is looking for people who aren't going to complain every time they are asked to do something. He is looking for people who refuse to have to be begged but are the first ones to jump up and volunteer to be a part of whatever their youth pastor or pastor needs from them.

As a WorldChanger, you need to spend some time every day or every week doing something specific to expand the kingdom of God. Use your sweat and labor to do something to assist your youth pastor or your pastor, and make it a part of your life. It shouldn't be a rare occurrence. It shouldn't just happen now and then when there is a special activity. You should determine, "I have to use my energy for God this week. I have to use at least some of it in a direct way to expand the kingdom of God and to serve as the disciples served Jesus."

Do you have anything on your calendar this week to use your energy for God? Make plans right now so you don't waste any more of your energy on just doing worldly things.

Everyone Has a Job to Do

EPHESIANS 4:16
FROM HIM THE WHOLE BODY, JOINED AND HELD TOGETHER BY EVERY
SUPPORTING LIGAMENT, GROWS AND BUILDS ITSELF UP IN LOVE, AS EACH PART
DOES ITS WORK.

I n this passage, Paul is equating the body of Christ with the physical body. There are many parts of the physical body: arms, legs, hands, and so forth. Every part is important. Paul goes on to say that when each part does its work, all parts work together. In other words, each part of the body has a job to do.

As a member of the body of Christ, you have a job to do, too. You were specially created by God to do a specific thing that will expand the kingdom of God because of the skills, personality, and relationships He has given you. And you feel totally and radically fulfilled only when you do the work that you were created to do. You weren't created to have a "the work of the Lord is my burden" mentality. Work is supposed to be a blessing.

You were created to do something. When you find what you were created to do and you start doing that work, it's the best kind of sweat you can ever expend because you go to bed at night knowing that you worked hard and that your work counted for something. Then you can't wait to get up the next day because you look forward to making your life and your work count again for the kingdom of God.

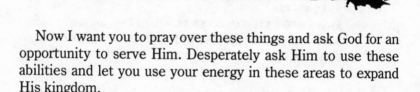 What kind of work do you think you were created for? Take a few minutes here and think about the giftings, talents, and desires that God has put inside you. List some of them here. What kind of work could you do that would really be a blessing to the kingdom of God or to your pastor or youth pastor?

—— ———— ———————— ——— ——————

—— ———— ———— ———— ——————

—— ———— ———— ——

Now I want you to pray over these things and ask God for an opportunity to serve Him. Desperately ask Him to use these abilities and let you use your energy in these areas to expand His kingdom.

Now go and talk to your pastor and youth pastor. Tell them that you think you have these things to offer and ask them if there is anywhere you could possibly use them to expand His kingdom or to expand the vision of the church.

Work for Lasting Results

JOHN 6:27
DO NOT WORK FOR FOOD THAT SPOILS, BUT FOR FOOD THAT ENDURES TO
ETERNAL LIFE, WHICH THE SON OF MAN WILL GIVE YOU. ON HIM GOD THE
FATHER HAS PLACED HIS SEAL OF APPROVAL.

1 CORINTHIANS 9:1
AM I NOT FREE? AM I NOT AN APOSTLE? HAVE I NOT SEEN JESUS OUR
LORD? ARE YOU NOT THE RESULT OF MY WORK IN THE LORD?

In these two Scriptures you can definitely see the difference
in two kinds of work. Describe that difference, in your own
words, based on these two Scriptures.

John 6:27: _____

_____

_____

1 Corinthians 9:1: _____ _____ _____ _____

_____ _____ _____ _____ _____

_____ _____ _____ _____ _____

Jesus encourages us not to work for food that spoils. Don't let your labor count only for something that is going to get thrown away. So what if you earn or build a bunch of stuff or have all the stuff the world says is so awesome? If that's the only thing that

MISSIONS IS...
seeing people through
Jesus' eyes and loving
them the same.
—Dee

your energies are going for, it's all going to get thrown away. It's all going to burn. That kind of work is totally unfulfilling because you end up with the stuff and then realize it doesn't make a difference. That doesn't mean it's wrong to have stuff. God wants to bless our lives. The Bible says that the favor of the Lord brings blessing, and He adds no trouble to it (Prov. 10:22). It means that you can get blessed and have stuff, but you won't have the trouble of the world.

The second kind of work is described in 1 Corinthians 9. Paul says, "Are you not the result of my work?" In other words, Paul and his helpers worked hard. They hiked to the villages. They had to make their own tents and earn their own money so they wouldn't have to ask for money from anybody. Then they preached, discipled, and set up Bible studies. They also held more follow-up meetings and kept working and working and working. As a result of their physical work, lives were radically changed. Churches were started, and lives were eternally different because of their sweat.

Your choice today as a WorldChanger is to choose what you are going to let your sweat count for. So what if you get your own car. So what if you can even pay the insurance on your car. So what if you sweat really hard and your ball team goes to the championship. In the realm of eternity, does it really matter if you go to the championship? I know these things are fun. It isn't that they are wrong, but at least some of your energies should go toward doing things that count for eternity, things that make a difference in the long run.

As a result of your choices this week, you ought to be able to look back and say, "Are you not the result of my work?" just as Paul did. In other words, lives should be touched and people should be changed as a result of the work you do. This nation should be different because of the work you do. Your school should be different because of the work you do. Something should be changed for eternity because of your work.

Determine now that you're going to make this week, and every week, end with having accomplished something significant for God. Refuse to go through one more week, one more month, one more year of your life without being able to say, "You are the fruit of my labor for the kingdom of God." Determine to be somebody who works hard for the King.

God Is Your Judge

1 PETER 1:17
SINCE YOU CALL ON A FATHER WHO JUDGES EACH MAN'S WORK IMPARTIALLY,
LIVE YOUR LIVES AS STRANGERS HERE IN REVERENT FEAR.

HEBREWS 6:10
GOD IS NOT UNJUST; HE WILL NOT FORGET YOUR WORK AND THE LOVE YOU HAVE
SHOWN HIM AS YOU HAVE HELPED HIS PEOPLE AND CONTINUE TO HELP THEM.

We're talking this week about having the character trait of being a hard worker. We're talking about developing a strong work ethic and being conscientious about what you do. Do things right even when people aren't watching over your shoulder every single minute of the day. I want you to see that the Bible is clear that God judges your work. You shouldn't be concerned as much about what Mom and Dad, teachers, pastors, or anyone else will say about your work. God is going to judge your work. He is going to decide if your heart was pure, if you did your very best, and if you were conscientious. As you work as for God, you know that He is your immediate supervisor. He is the One who is going to check out your work.

It also says that God doesn't forget your work. Once you've done something for God, it's not forgotten. The only work that is forgotten is work that is done for temporal reasons, but if you work for the kingdom, you do something that counts for eternity. God will never, ever forget what you do. And neither will the people who were helped or ministered to or changed because of your work.

Work isn't just a little extracurricular activity for God. It's a holy thing. God worked when He made this world. He commanded Adam to work the Garden (and, yes, that was *before* the curse). Now He is looking to us as WorldChangers to work at something that counts. That is what people in this generation are looking for—something they can work for that matters.

Working for the kingdom of God is really the only thing that matters. We need to be sure that we don't end up like the people in Revelation 2—they did a bunch of work, but they forgot their first love. We want to make sure that our passion for God is right and that our yearning for the reality of the living Christ inside us is always there. When our passion is for God, we desire to use our hearts, lives, and energy to do something so that other people can get connected to the very real Christ we are connected to.

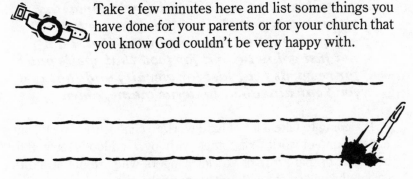

Take a few minutes here and list some things you have done for your parents or for your church that you know God couldn't be very happy with.

— — —— — —— — —— — —— —— — —— ——

— — —— — —— — —— — —— — —— ——

— — —— — —— — —— — —— —— —

Now list some things you've done that you're really proud of. List things that you don't want God to forget because you know that you did your very best and they are counting for eternity. It could be a project at church, an outreach with the youth group, a mission trip, or anything else you know you did well.

Take some time and pray about what you've just done. Say,

Lord, thank You that You don't forget these things, these labors of love that I've done for You. Thank You, Lord, that lives have been changed as a result. Amen.

Now make a commitment to the Lord about the kind of person you want to be. Say,

Lord, I commit to be a hard worker. For the rest of my life I will use my energy, my sweat, my toil, my brain, and my body in some way, either big or small. I am going to use my energy to expand the kingdom of God. I am not just going to do it for food that spoils but for rewards that last for eternity and that are for Your kingdom. In Jesus' name, amen.

It's going to take a lot of hard work to change this world, but it's the kind of work that comes with joy. God looks for you to be a part of that army of WorldChangers who are not afraid to sweat and will sweat with joy because they know their sweat is counting for eternity.

WEEK 11

Vision

Challenge 9:
WorldChangers Start a Revolution

God Believes in You

LUKE 5:10
JESUS SAID TO SIMON, "DON'T BE AFRAID; FROM NOW ON YOU WILL CATCH
MEN."

Take a few moments to read through Luke 5:1–11. What do you think is the significance of what Jesus told Simon Peter: "From now on you will catch men"? What did He really mean?

I want you to picture the kind of guy Peter was. He was a fisherman—a hardworking guy, but not necessarily very talented. He had a lot of muscles, but he was not necessarily very smart. His hair was probably a little matted. He was most likely sweaty and stinky and probably hadn't had a bath in a few days. Because fishermen weren't rich in those days and didn't have much status, he probably had a beat-up boat. But when Jesus asked him to go fishing, all of a sudden a miracle happened. After a full night of fishing and catching nothing, Peter filled up his boat and his friends' boat. He came back to Jesus and said, "Go away from me, Lord; I am a sinful man!"

Jesus spoke some words to Peter that forever changed his life. He said, "Peter, you're going to be a fisher of men." Jesus was making a remark about Peter's potential, about what He could see Peter doing. In essence, He was saying, "Peter, I can see the future and I can see what God has in store for you. You're going to preach to three thousand people someday. Peter, you're going to lay hands on that man at the Gate Beautiful, and he is going to be healed. In fact, Peter, you're going to contribute to a book that will be on the best-seller list longer than any other book in the history of the world." Jesus believed in Peter.

Vision is a key element if you're going to start a revolution in your hometown. It is strategically linked to the ninth challenge of a WorldChanger. I want to encourage you today to begin to dream, begin to let God stir you up with His vision. Dare to dream big.

Peter was thinking about fish; Jesus was thinking about men. Peter was thinking about the Sea of Galilee; Jesus was thinking about the world. Let God stimulate your dreaming ability now. Dream big. Think big. Have a big vision for your school, your community, your world, and your life. Ask the Lord right now,

God, if You had Your very best, what could You do in me and through me to change the world? In Jesus' name, amen.

The Big Picture

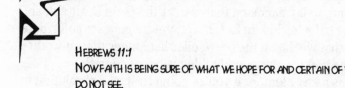

HEBREWS 11:1
NOW FAITH IS BEING SURE OF WHAT WE HOPE FOR AND CERTAIN OF WHAT WE
DO NOT SEE.

Write out in 1990s teenage lingo what you think this verse means.

We're talking this week about having vision as a World-Changer: being full of vision and seeing more than the average person can see, seeing the big picture. Don't be confined by what you see physically. Get a glimpse of what God wants to have happen, and do everything you can to be a part of making it happen.

The Bible talks about having faith. Some people in the world are constantly negative. Anytime you bring up a big idea to them, they tell you all the reasons why it can't work. God is looking for visionaries who are full of faith. As soon as WorldChangers hear an idea or get a dream

MISSIONS HAS GIUEN ME...
boldness and purpose.
—Kat & Sherman

from God, they have confidence that God can make it happen. They see something in the Scripture, and they know that it's true. They know they can succeed because the Bible says they can.

I want to encourage you today to take Hebrews 11:1 and meditate on it all day long. Let God build confidence in you as a WorldChanger that what He said in the Word is true and He will complete it. If you're going to change the world, you have to have confidence in the face of any circumstance that God's Word is true, and nothing will stop you from completing what He told you to do. When everybody else says things can't be done or they seem impossible, you have to be the one who is the World-Changer, who sees the big picture of God's vision and has great confidence that what God wants to have happen is going to happen. Faith is being confident in what you hope for, being confident in what you know God says is going to happen and not wavering.

God Is for You

Romans 8:31, 38-39

If God is for us, who can be against us? ... For I am convinced that neither death nor life, neither angels nor demons, neither the present nor the future, nor any powers, neither height nor depth, nor anything else in all creation, will be able to separate us from the love of God that is in Christ Jesus our Lord.

Take five minutes to memorize these verses right now. We're talking this week about being a person of vision. A WorldChanger has to have God's vision. Somebody with vision is somebody who is positive, somebody who can see the best in any situation. A WorldChanger has to be somebody who can see a way to get through any hindrance that would stop her from accomplishing what God has called her to do. There are two kinds of people in the world: people who always see the negative side of things and people who always see the positive side. A WorldChanger sees the positive and knows that he will succeed no matter what. A WorldChanger believes that not only is God on his side, but God will cause everything to work together for his good.

You can have confidence that the dream God has put in your heart will come to pass. This Scripture says that if God is for you, no one can be against you. Nothing can separate you from the love of God. Nothing can pull you away from His favor on your life if you keep your heart pure.

A WorldChanger has an overarching positive passion. This positive attitude spreads into every conversation, every relationship, so that it becomes contagious. People will feel that not only can you do anything you put your mind to, but others can also do anything because there is such a positive sense of encouragement in everything you as a WorldChanger say and do. A WorldChanger sees no barrier as unsurpassable. Nothing is impossible to someone who believes.

Think about some areas right now that you haven't been very positive about. List them here.

Think about how you can change your attitude in these areas so that next time you talk about them or think about them you'll be able to attack them with a WorldChanger's positive attitude.

Week 11

DAY 4

That All Would Be Saved

1 TIMOTHY 2:4

[GOD] WANTS ALL MEN TO BE SAVED AND TO COME TO A KNOWLEDGE OF THE TRUTH.

ake four minutes to memorize this verse. Write it out on an index card so you can carry it with you all day. As you have been learning this week, a WorldChanger is someone with vision. Vision is stimulated and stirred up by the Word of God. This Scripture exposes one of the most essential passions in the heart of God—that everyone would be saved and come to a knowledge of the truth. When God says *all*, He means *all*. He won't be satisfied with just a few people; He wants all people.

This vision inspires WorldChangers. They constantly look for ways to be used by God to affect all people. They pray about it. They think about it. They live for it. They want to do something to attain God's ultimate goal of reaching all people.

You need to let this Scripture get underneath your skin. You need to let it start beating in your heart so that in every realm of life—missions, your hometown, school, work—you start seeing God's heart and compassion for all people. Everything you do or say will come from the fact that God wants all people to be saved.

Write the names of some people you know who need to get saved.

First Timothy 2:4 is not just a neat little Scripture that happens to be in the Bible. It's the very heartbeat and passion of the living God. There is nobody beyond His reach and nobody He doesn't want to reach. There is nobody that His Son's blood wasn't shed for. As a WorldChanger, you see and embrace that and extend your vision to be enveloped in God's vision that all people will be saved. Begin now to pray for people you see every day to be saved.

MISSIONS HAS GIVEN ME...
joy.
—Amanda

God's Heart for the World

REVELATION 7:9
AFTER THIS I LOOKED AND THERE BEFORE ME WAS A GREAT MULTITUDE
THAT NO ONE COULD COUNT, FROM EVERY NATION, TRIBE, PEOPLE AND
LANGUAGE, STANDING BEFORE THE THRONE AND IN FRONT OF THE LAMB.
THEY WERE WEARING WHITE ROBES AND WERE HOLDING PALM BRANCHES
IN THEIR HANDS.

ake three minutes to memorize this Scripture.
Write it on an index card and carry the card
around so you can meditate on it. Why do you
think this Scripture is so important?

_____ _____ _____ _____

_____ _____ _____ _____

_____ _____ _____ _____

We're talking this week about being a person with vision. If you're really going to change the world, you have to expand your vision to get a glimpse of God's vision. God's vision reaches around the world to the ends of the earth. We see in the Scripture that God's heart for the world is complete. He starts off wanting the world. In the end of the Bible, He says, "I get some of each tribe, each nation, each language."

The point is that as a WorldChanger, you have to let the bigness of God's vision influence your vision. You have to think globally, think about the big picture, and sense God's heart. Whether or not you go and live on the mission field is not the issue. The issue is understanding the bigness of God's vision and that somehow the things you do with your life have to point to God's vision.

You need to meditate and chew on this principle all day long. God's heart for every tongue, every tribe, and every nation is an essential part of what makes Him tick. We're thinking about all the busyness in life—all our activities, sports, fun, and games. He is thinking about the end of the earth. He is thinking about the tribes that never had a chance. We need to let His heart for the whole world begin to color our vision so we think bigger, we pray bigger, we live bigger, and we inspire other people bigger. Our dream, our vision, must begin to encompass the world because that's what God's dream has done.

Let's Get Personal

We're talking about having a vision as a WorldChanger. Today, we want to talk about having a vision for your personal walk with God. You've memorized and meditated on several Scriptures this week. Now I want you to personalize what you've learned about being a WorldChanger and having vision.

It's important for you to have a game plan in your walk with God. Don't just go from day to day doing the best you can for Jesus. Take some time today during your quiet time, and begin to make a plan for the next year of your life by answering these questions.

Where would you like to be a year from now in your walk with God?

_____

_____

_____

In what areas of your life that you feel are a little bit weak now would you like to develop and get strong?

___ ___ ___ ___ ___ ___ ___

___ ___ ___ ___ ___ ___ ___

___ ___ ___ ___ ___ ___

What books, other than the Bible, would you like to read this year that would help you grow in the Lord?

___ ___ ___ ___ ___ ___ ___

___ ___ ___ ___ ___ ___ ___

___ ___ ___ ___ ___ ___

What areas of character would you like to develop in your life?

___ ___ ___ ___ ___ ___ ___

___ ___ ___ ___ ___ ___ ___

___ ___ ___ ___ ___ ___

MISSIONS IS...
being stretched.
—Greta

How much time would you like to spend praying in the next twelve months?

— — — — — — —

— — — — — — —

— — — — — — —

Can you think of a Bible hero you would love to become like over the course of the next year?

— — — — — — —

— — — — — — —

— — — — — — —

MISSIONS IS...
people.
—Sarah

How much of the Bible would you like to read next year? Or how many times would you like to read through the Bible in the next twelve months?

_____

_____

_____

What are you going to do to pursue these goals and start working toward them right now?

_____

_____

_____

Now I want you to take the ideas and thoughts that you have just written down here and pray over them all and consecrate them to the Lord today. Let God stimulate your vision for your personal life, and begin to chart a course to pursue the vision that you have here. Constantly update this vision for where you want your personal walk with the Lord to go. Otherwise you will one day find yourself stuck in a rut—just going to church and doing what you think you are supposed to do but feeling dry inside. God bless you as you jump out into your adventure and your walk with Him this year.

Your Ministry

> HABAKKUK 2:2
> WRITE DOWN THE REVELATION
> AND MAKE IT PLAIN ON TABLETS
> SO THAT A HERALD MAY RUN WITH IT.

That is exactly what you did yesterday—you wrote down your vision for your personal life. As a WorldChanger, you have to have a vision, both for your personal life and for the world. And today as you push through and become somebody who thinks big, dreams big, and plans big in every area of your life, I want you to think about the vision that God has for you right now. Yesterday we talked about vision for your personal life. Now I want you to think about vision for your ministry life. For example, what's your vision for your town? Think about it this way: If you did everything that Jesus wants you to do in the next six months or year, what would your town look like? What would your school look like if Jesus were a student right now? What would it look like in six months? What would it look like in a year?

_____ _____ _____ _____ _____ _____

_____ _____ _____ _____ _____

_____ _____ _____ _____ _____

I want you to start thinking about your career. Even though you might be only fourteen or sixteen, start thinking about God's plan for your life. What is your vision? How does God want to use you? Don't think small as Peter did when he was just thinking about fish. Start thinking about the world and how God wants to use you there. Write down some of the plans of the things that you always thought you'd do or become once you grew up.

_____ _____ _____ _____ _____ _____

_____ _____ _____ _____ _____

_____ _____ _____ _____ _____

Now dream a little. What kind of ministry do you think God might want you to be involved in? Everybody has to be involved in ministry—whether it is full-time or not is not the issue. You may not be called to be a preacher, but everybody is called to expand the kingdom of God. How do you think He might want you to do that?

_____ _____ _____ _____ _____ _____

_____ _____ _____ _____ _____

_____ _____ _____ _____ _____

How do you plan to get there? For example, do you need to go to a college or university? Which one? What should you major in? Just write down how you think God wants you to begin to fulfill your vision. Remember, don't let money or location keep you from dreaming big. God wants you to be the very best so you can accomplish the very best for His kingdom.

Take some time to pray over all these plans. Don't take them lightly, and don't just skip over this and go to the next day. I want you to think through each of these. The Bible says you have to write down the vision and make it plain. Make it clear so that you can have a sense of direction for where God wants you to go. And pursue it with all of your heart.

As a WorldChanger, you are going to see not just the trees but the forest. You'll see the big picture. God is looking for young people with a big vision, the big picture of where He is calling them to go. He can't as effectively use people who are wandering aimlessly through life. God will use people who know exactly the path that He has laid out for them and who are going to do everything they can to pursue it with all of their hearts.

WEEK 12

Endurance

Challenge 10:

WorldChangers Go on a Mission Trip
While They're Teens

The End

MATTHEW 24:4-14

JESUS ANSWERED: "WATCH OUT THAT NO ONE DECEIVES YOU. FOR MANY
WILL COME IN MY NAME, CLAIMING, 'I AM THE CHRIST,' AND WILL DECEIVE
MANY. YOU WILL HEAR OF WARS AND RUMORS OF WARS, BUT SEE TO IT THAT
YOU ARE NOT ALARMED. SUCH THINGS MUST HAPPEN, BUT THE END IS STILL TO
COME. NATION WILL RISE AGAINST NATION, AND KINGDOM AGAINST KINGDOM.
THERE WILL BE FAMINES AND EARTHQUAKES IN VARIOUS PLACES. ALL THESE ARE
THE BEGINNING OF BIRTH PAINS. THEN YOU WILL BE HANDED OVER TO BE
PERSECUTED AND PUT TO DEATH, AND YOU WILL BE HATED BY ALL NATIONS
BECAUSE OF ME. AT THAT TIME MANY WILL TURN AWAY FROM THE FAITH AND
WILL BETRAY AND HATE EACH OTHER, AND MANY FALSE PROPHETS WILL APPEAR
AND DECEIVE MANY PEOPLE. BECAUSE OF THE INCREASE OF WICKEDNESS, THE
LOVE OF MOST WILL GROW COLD, <u>BUT HE WHO STANDS FIRM TO THE END WILL BE
SAVED. AND THIS GOSPEL OF THE KINGDOM WILL BE PREACHED IN THE WHOLE
WORLD AS A TESTIMONY TO ALL NATIONS, AND THEN THE END WILL COME.</u>"

 Take a few minutes now to memorize Matthew
24:13–14 (underlined).

What kinds of things did Jesus say would happen at the end?

_____ _____ _____ _____ _____ _____

_____ _____ _____ _____ _____ _____

_____ _____ _____ _____ _____

How are we to respond?

_____ _____ _____ _____ _____ _____

_____ _____ _____ _____ _____

_____ _____ _____ _____

The final point of character we are going to talk about is endurance. In this passage Jesus is helping the disciples in the early days of the church understand what the end times are going to be like. He talks about all of the persecution and the bad things that are going to happen. Then He says that all who will stand firm, who will endure to the end, will be saved. God is looking for people who will endure, who will fight the good fight of faith and are in it for the long haul. He is looking for people who are not just in it when things are going well but who will stay when things are going bad as well.

Those who will endure to the end will be saved. To the end of what? To the end of high school? No. To the end of college? No. To the end of the year? No. Those who endure to *the end of the end* will be saved. This enduring thing is not a matter of, "Well, maybe if you're a really good Christian, you can do it." According to this Scripture, the only people who are going to be saved are those who endure. God wants to build in us a supernatural resilience so that we can handle anything and we can endure no matter what.

Then in verse 14, Jesus says that the gospel will be preached throughout the world, then the end will come. Watch this. Jesus is telling the disciples about all the persecution that is going to happen and that only those who endure through all that are going to be saved, but *they shouldn't get freaked out because that's not the end yet.* Then He says, "In the midst of all this stuff that is going on, in spite of all the bad things happening around the world, one thing is going to stay consistent—My gospel is going to keep going out to the ends of My earth until all of the nations know. It's going out to all the people who never had a chance, then the end will come." In other words, don't get freaked out by everything going on around you. *You have to endure.* And in the midst of all the crises, keep reaching out to the people around the world who have never had a chance to hear about God.

Let me put it to you this way: You have to endure to the end because you have to reach this world. The character trait of endurance is directly linked to challenge 10, which is going on a mission trip sometime while you are a teenager. If you're going to change the world, you're going to have to get out there and reach the people. It's going to take some endurance and perseverance to do it because those who endure to the end will be saved. And in the midst of everything the people who are enduring are going to be reaching out to the world. They are going to be ministering. They are not just going to be hanging out, hanging on to a rope somewhere, hoping to endure. They are going to be rocking and shaking this world right until the very end.

MISSIONS IS...
hard work.
—Jon

God needs some people who will put the character trait of endurance into their lives and who will say, "Lord, no matter what it takes, no matter how hard it is, I'm going to reach the world. No matter how many beans I have to eat, how hard the floor is, how hard it is to raise the money, I'm going to endure until the end. I'm not a fair-weather Christian. I'm not just going to reach the world if it is convenient, fun, or exciting. I'll reach it if no one else wants to do it. I'll do it because You want to do it, Lord, and I want to please You."

If you have not yet made a commitment to go on a mission trip, right now is the time to do it. Maybe you made a commitment, but the commitment didn't endure. You got overwhelmed by other things. Right now is the time to slam on the brakes and say, "Lord, even if I go only one time, would You really have me go?" Then commit to endure to the end to do whatever it takes to raise the money, to get out there, and to do it. Jesus says those who endure to the end will be saved, and while they're enduring, they're going to be reaching the world. Right now is the time to jump in to be the kind of Christian who endures until the end.

Press On

PHILIPPIANS 3:12-14

NOT THAT I HAVE ALREADY OBTAINED ALL THIS, OR HAVE ALREADY BEEN MADE PERFECT, BUT I PRESS ON TO TAKE HOLD OF THAT FOR WHICH CHRIST JESUS TOOK HOLD OF ME. BROTHERS, I DO NOT CONSIDER MYSELF YET TO HAVE TAKEN HOLD OF IT. BUT ONE THING I DO: FORGETTING WHAT IS BEHIND AND STRAINING TOWARD WHAT IS AHEAD, I PRESS ON TOWARD THE GOAL TO WIN THE PRIZE FOR WHICH GOD HAS CALLED ME HEAVENWARD IN CHRIST JESUS.

Take five minutes to memorize and meditate on this Scripture. Write out what you think it means for you today.

_____

_____

_____

When I was a young Christian, this was one of my favorite Scriptures. Every time I heard those words, "Press on, press on," I got a brand-new burst of fire in my heart to keep going after God. God is looking for an army of people who will press on, who will keep enduring.

Paul wouldn't look at his past. He had some pretty bad failures in his past. He had killed Christians and fought hard against the kingdom of God. And he had some pretty great successes in his past, too. He had seen incredible revivals. But he didn't look back at his past, either the failures or the successes. He looked ahead and pressed on. He endured to the end.

What did he mean when he said, "I take hold of that for which Christ Jesus took hold of me"? He was trying to figure out why Jesus had grabbed hold of him so he could do everything God had called him to do before he died. When Paul wrote this letter, he had been in the ministry for a long time. But he kept saying, "I'm still trying to figure out every single thing He wants me to do so I can be sure to do it all. I'm pressing on and pressing on and pressing on. I'm not giving up. I'm not looking back at failures or successes. I'm looking ahead."

Take this Scripture with you all day long and meditate on it. Commit to the Lord right now. Say,

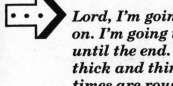

Lord, I'm going to be one of those who press on. I'm going to be one of those who endure until the end. I'm going to press on through thick and thin. When times are hard, when times are rough, I'm going to hang on to the very end. I will press on and accomplish everything You have called me to do on this earth. In Jesus' name, amen.

When the Going Gets Tough

1 CORINTHIANS 4:12
WE WORK HARD WITH OUR OWN HANDS. WHEN WE ARE CURSED, WE BLESS;
WHEN WE ARE PERSECUTED, WE ENDURE IT.

2 TIMOTHY 2:5
IF ANYONE COMPETES AS AN ATHLETE, HE DOES NOT RECEIVE THE VICTOR'S
CROWN UNLESS HE COMPETES ACCORDING TO THE RULES.

HEBREWS 12:7
ENDURE HARDSHIP AS DISCIPLINE; GOD IS TREATING YOU AS SONS. FOR WHAT
SON IS NOT DISCIPLINED BY HIS FATHER?

What do these passages of Scripture have in common?

_____

_____

_____

We are talking about endurance this week. Paul had a kind of resilience that no matter what came against him, he would press on. He was determined to persevere. When he was persecuted, he would endure it as a soldier of the Lord. Any hardship he faced—having no food, having to walk long distances between villages, or having no place to sleep—he endured it as a soldier. Think about military soldiers. They will go through anything they have to do to win the war, to get the job done. Yet too many of us Christians think if it gets a little bit hard, it must not be of the Lord.

The book of Hebrews says that we endure hardship as discipline. Tough times help us stay more focused on the Lord. They help us realize how messed up the world is so we will stay away from its snares. As soon as they endure something hard or go through a tough time, some people are weakened in their faith. They might think, *God doesn't love me anymore,* or *So what? I've been a Christian. Look what it got me.* Well, look what it got Paul! It got him incredible victories, but it also got him incredible persecutions.

It is time for a new generation of young people to stand up and say, "You know what? I don't care what I have to go through for the Lord. I don't care if it's hard. I don't care if it's easy. It just doesn't matter. I know He loves me. I've given my life to Him and what I've got inside me is real. I don't care what I have to go through, I'm hanging on. And not only am I hanging on, but I'm going to grab some arms and take some people with me. I'm not going to just barely make it to heaven. I'm going to endure as a soldier. I'm going to stay strong. I'm going to keep my shoulders back and my chin up high."

The Bible tells us not to get freaked out when persecutions or hard times come our way. Let's get excited because Jesus had the same kinds of persecutions and He endured. If He endured, He will give you the strength to endure as well. But you've got to decide you're going to do it no matter what.

Through the Fire

Romans 5:3 – 4

WE ALSO REJOICE IN OUR SUFFERINGS, BECAUSE WE KNOW THAT SUFFERING PRODUCES PERSEVERANCE; PERSEVERANCE, CHARACTER; AND CHARACTER, HOPE.

This passage describes the fact that persecution, and perseverance in that persecution, will produce character. It's like making a sword. The blacksmith gets the metal really hot, and then he dips it in water. He gets it red hot again and then plunges it back into the water. He keeps repeating this process until the sword is so strong that almost nothing can crack, chip, or break it in any way. It is practically indestructible. That's what God wants to do in us. When we go through intense times, we are going through the fire. When we get full of the Word of God, we are getting cooled off. We go through the fire, and we get cooled off. When we repeatedly go through this cycle, we become so strong and so resilient that nothing the devil does, nothing he tries to shove in our faces, can mess up our walk with God. That process produces character in our lives. That sword is strong. It virtually cannot be busted, chipped, or bent. That's the kind of character you need to have.

When you persevere and endure in the midst of tough times, you get stronger and stronger. You become more resilient, more committed, more full of faith, more confident than you have ever been in your life. You might be only fourteen or fifteen years old, but you can have incredible strength inside you.

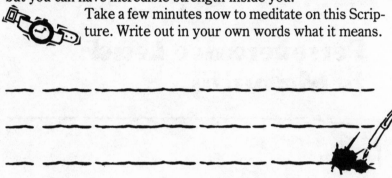
Take a few minutes now to meditate on this Scripture. Write out in your own words what it means.

— —— ——— —— ——— —— ——— —

— —— ——— —— ——— —— ———

— —— ——— —— ——— —— ———

You know, some people have been in church their whole lives. In fact, they have grown gray in the church, but they're weak. They have no character. They haven't endured. They have repeatedly compromised their standards. It's time for you to show yourself an example. Show that when tough times come, you're going to endure. And in the process of enduring, you'll be reaching out to change the world all along the way as Jesus described in Matthew 24.

Perseverance Leads to Maturity

JAMES 1:2 – 4
CONSIDER IT PURE JOY, MY BROTHERS, WHENEVER YOU FACE TRIALS OF MANY KINDS, BECAUSE YOU KNOW THAT THE TESTING OF YOUR FAITH DEVELOPS PERSEVERANCE. PERSEVERANCE MUST FINISH ITS WORK SO THAT YOU MAY BE MATURE AND COMPLETE, NOT LACKING ANYTHING.

W rite out this Scripture in your 1990s teenage version of what you think it means.

The key line I want you to focus on is how perseverance, when it has finished its work, produces maturity. God is looking for some mature men and women of God. You don't have to be old to be mature. There are some old, very immature Christians. They think they're mature because they have heard all the Bible stories and been at church all their lives. But God doesn't measure maturity by the number of years at church or by the number of years in Christ. He measures maturity by obedience. How obedient are you to Christ? How much have you persevered?

The Bible says that when you persevere, when you endure, when you keep enduring and enduring and persevering and going after God no matter what, its completion produces maturity. It produces strength. It produces character. You become like a pillar that cannot be moved.

In today's church, and especially in today's youth groups, you don't see enough mature young men and women of God, even though many members have been in church for a long time. Now is the time to start persevering, to start building a habit of persevering, that no matter what, you're going to let perseverance finish its work in you. Don't just persevere to the end of the week or to the end of the year or to the end of camp or until you get on your mission trip. Persevere to the end. It will produce maturity in you.

One reason mission trips are so great is that you have to persevere just to get to the mission field—raising your money, praying like crazy, and watching God do all the miracles to get your money in there. You persevere, and you plan. You buy everything you need to go. Then you finally get on the trip and you have to persevere some more! You have to work hard. You sweat hard doing the drama, ministering, learning a new language, and eating food you don't like. You learn to persevere. You learn that this gospel, and spreading this gospel, is worth persevering for.

When you come back, you're more mature. Perseverance has its perfect work in you and produces maturity. When you go through an experience like that, you see some other people around you, and you see the games they play in their Christian lives. And you realize you don't want to have any part of that kind of life. You have maturity built into your life because you've persevered.

Persevere in Victory

> **2 PETER 1:5–7**
> MAKE EVERY EFFORT TO ADD TO YOUR FAITH GOODNESS; AND TO GOODNESS,
> KNOWLEDGE; AND TO KNOWLEDGE, SELF-CONTROL: AND TO SELF-CONTROL,
> PERSEVERANCE; AND TO PERSEVERANCE, GODLINESS; AND TO GODLINESS,
> BROTHERLY KINDNESS; AND TO BROTHERLY KINDNESS, LOVE.

 We used this passage earlier, but I want you to see the order of progression here. Take a few minutes right now to make sure that you still have these verses memorized. We talked about adding self-control to your knowledge—that the more things you learn, the more controlled you are. You learned all about self-control. Now, it says, add perseverance to your self-control. Once you've started controlling yourself, controlling your lust, controlling your flesh, controlling your mind, and controlling your body, add perseverance to that. In other words, keep controlling. Don't just control yourself for a week or for a month.

Some people get one victory, and they think they are completely self-controlled over some sin in their lives for a month or so. But then they fall back into their old habits again. The Bible tells us to add perseverance to that one victory. Get locked in and say, "This is going to be my lifestyle! I'm going to persevere in these areas of self-control. I'm controlling my life and persevering in the things that I've learned."

List some areas in your life where you've had recent victories and now you need to concentrate on persevering in the victories.

The Bible says to add perseverance to your self-control. In other words, it's a choice you make. It's like a building block. You're building one thing upon another. After you've done all these things, add perseverance. You have the recipe for a successful Christian life. You have all the ingredients down. Now persevere. Build perseverance into your life. Build the kind of character that says, "No matter what, I'm not a quitter. I'm not going to stop. I'm going to persevere!" God will give you the strength. He'll give you the power, but you have to make the decision to persevere.

Week **12**

DAY **7**

The Promise

REVELATION 3:10
SINCE YOU HAVE KEPT MY COMMAND TO ENDURE PATIENTLY, I WILL ALSO KEEP YOU FROM THE HOUR OF TRIAL THAT IS GOING TO COME UPON THE WHOLE WORLD TO TEST THOSE WHO LIVE ON THE EARTH.

HEBREWS 10:36
YOU NEED TO PERSEVERE SO THAT WHEN YOU HAVE DONE THE WILL OF GOD, YOU WILL RECEIVE WHAT HE HAS PROMISED.

List the two promises here that you can expect as a result of persevering.

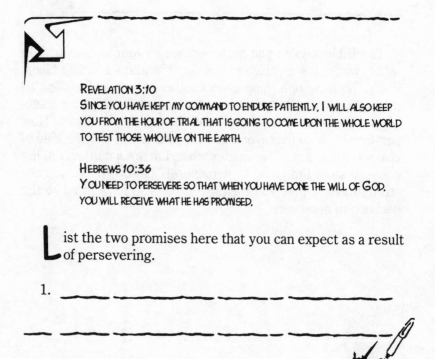

1. _____

_____

_____

2. _____

_____

_____

You can see in Revelation that God promises to keep you from the hour of trial. In other words, if you show your perseverance, your tenacity to stick to Him no matter what, the Lord will protect you when the devil comes and wants to put you on trial to grill you and mess you up. God won't allow you to be tempted more than you could possibly bear (1 Cor. 10:13). God will not take advantage of you. He wants to protect you from the hour of trial. He just wants to know that you would go through it if you needed to.

You might need to go through a tough time now and then, but don't worry. Show your perseverance and God will protect you. You have to continue to endure to receive the promise of the Father, that is, eternal life.

Let me tell you what endurance produces. Endurance produces strong Christians, but it also produces Christians who change the world. They realize that they are not just here to persevere, just to say they made it to the end. They are here to persevere so that they can make a difference in and really change this world.

Endurance is not just enduring so you can live a long life and then die. Endurance is persevering so you can make an impact on your world. Endurance is hanging on till the end. It's wanting to live a long life

MISSIONS IS...
fulfilling God's dream.
—Jacob

of faithfulness to the Lord so you can use your long life to continue to have an effect on this world.

The only reason for us to stay in this world is to make a difference. If God didn't want to use us, we'd have been raptured as soon as we got saved. You see, the whole idea of enduring is persevering so you can live a long life and affect this world for as long as you possibly can before you go home to see the Lord.

Make your life count now. Sign up to go on a mission trip this summer, and plan to endure until the end. Be a part of the army of young people who take all ten challenges and endure to the very end. Don't be a wallflower Christian. Don't just blend in. Build character in your life. Continue to live these challenges. Start making your life count now while you're young so you can establish a lifestyle of doing it for the rest of your life.

WEEK 13

Recap

What Is Character?

> **2 PETER 1:5–9**
> FOR THIS VERY REASON, MAKE EVERY EFFORT TO ADD TO YOUR FAITH
> GOODNESS; AND TO GOODNESS, KNOWLEDGE; AND TO KNOWLEDGE,
> SELF-CONTROL; AND TO SELF-CONTROL, PERSEVERANCE; AND TO PERSEVERANCE,
> GODLINESS; AND TO GODLINESS, BROTHERLY KINDNESS; AND TO BROTHERLY
> KINDNESS, LOVE. FOR IF YOU POSSESS THESE QUALITIES IN INCREASING MEASURE,
> THEY WILL KEEP YOU FROM BEING INEFFECTIVE AND UNPRODUCTIVE IN YOUR
> KNOWLEDGE OF OUR LORD JESUS CHRIST. BUT IF ANYONE DOES NOT HAVE
> THEM, HE IS NEARSIGHTED AND BLIND, AND HAS FORGOTTEN THAT HE HAS BEEN
> CLEANSED FROM HIS PAST SINS.

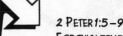 ake a few minutes to make sure you still have
this Scripture memorized.

What are the main things you've learned about character in
the last few weeks?

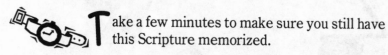

Why is character so important in a Christian's life?

_____ _____ _____ _____ _____ _____

_____ _____ _____ _____ _____ _____

_____ _____ _____ _____ _____ _____

In what areas of character do you feel that you've seen some real change in your life?

_____ _____ _____ _____ _____ _____

_____ _____ _____ _____ _____ _____

_____ _____ _____ _____ _____ _____

God wants to add things that will bring substance and credibility to your life when you choose to become a WorldChanger. That means people will believe what you say because of what they see in your life. That is what character is about—a collection of godly habits. When people look at you, they see a glimpse of your Father. It's not enough just to learn about character; you have to be a person of character. You have to apply character to your life and grow in character. You must constantly pursue character.

As you walk through your teen years, make this a mark on your life: If you do nothing else, pursue character with all your heart. Get the character of God deep down into the way you live. I want to encourage you today to be a Christian who is building character. Keep getting stronger in areas where you feel weak. Don't let building character end with this book. Let it be the beginning of a lifestyle that constantly strengthens your character.

Passion and Stability

Having *a passion for God* is definitely a mark of a World-Changer. Mark 12:29–30 talks about loving Him with all your heart.

> MARK 12:29–30
> "THE MOST IMPORTANT [COMMANDMENT]," ANSWERED JESUS, "IS THIS:
> 'HEAR, O ISRAEL, THE LORD OUR GOD, THE LORD IS ONE. LOVE THE LORD
> YOUR GOD WITH ALL YOUR HEART AND WITH ALL YOUR SOUL AND WITH ALL
> YOUR MIND AND WITH ALL YOUR STRENGTH.'"

This distinct mark of loving God ought to blow away everything else in your life. It ought to be what people see in you more than anything else. The first thing people should notice about you is that you have a passion for God and that you are not ashamed of it.

We also talked about having *stability*. We talked about not being a hype-oriented Christian, going back and forth based on whatever you feel but being determined to live a strong, stable Christian life.

1 Timothy 4:12

DON'T LET ANYONE LOOK DOWN ON YOU BECAUSE YOU ARE YOUNG, BUT SET AN EXAMPLE FOR THE BELIEVERS IN SPEECH, IN LIFE, IN LOVE, IN FAITH AND IN PURITY.

This Scripture talks about being an example even while you're young. Don't wait until you're old. Be an example now by the way you live. God is looking for young people who will be faithful, who will be stable. He is looking for young people He and other people can count on in this world.

MISSIONS IS...
fields of wheat waiting
to be harvested.
—Tasci

Today, I want you to take these two Scriptures—Mark 12:29–30 and 1 Timothy 4:12—and meditate on them all day long. Begin to practice these two character traits of having a passion for God so you love Him more than anything and being stable in the Lord.

Strength and Integrity

Strength is a character trait that you have to ingrain into your life.

1 JOHN 2:14
I WRITE TO YOU, YOUNG MEN,
BECAUSE YOU ARE STRONG,
AND THE WORD OF GOD LIVES IN YOU,
AND YOU HAVE OVERCOME THE EVIL ONE.

God is looking for men and women who are strong in the Lord. You get strong by cramming the Word of God into your mind and heart. A WorldChanger studies the Word of God on a daily basis. You don't just haphazardly read through the Bible because you know that's where your strength comes from.

We also talked about being people of *integrity*. Having integrity means that when we give our word, we keep our word.

This Scripture talks about having a good name or a good reputation. That means people can believe you when you say something. It's important to have an accountability friend who can help you really know if you are walking in integrity.

MISSIONS IS...
normal people in
everyday life.
—Josh & David

People with integrity are the same in private as in public. They are not fake Christians. They don't have to pretend that they are spiritual when they are not. People who have integrity honestly seek God with all their hearts. They do everything they can to establish a reputation that is really pleasing to God. World-Changers have integrity.

Take these two Scriptures today, and meditate on them all day. Think about things that you can do today to exude more strength, and practice integrity in everything you do, say, and think.

Self-Control and Purity

W e talked about having *self-control*.

GALATIANS 5:22-23
BUT THE FRUIT OF THE SPIRIT IS LOVE, JOY, PEACE, PATIENCE, KINDNESS, GOOD-
NESS, FAITHFULNESS, GENTLENESS AND SELF-CONTROL. AGAINST SUCH THINGS
THERE IS NO LAW.

You can see that self-control is one fruit of the Spirit. It's one thing that God wants to grow in your life. It demonstrates that God's Spirit is in you and has borne fruit. God gave you His Holy Spirit when you gave your life to Him. He has given you the power to be in control of your life. There is no sin, there is no demon, there is no temptation, that can force you or tell you what to do. *You* have the opportunity to dictate your destiny.

We also talked about having *a pure heart*.

MATTHEW 5:8
BLESSED ARE THE PURE IN HEART,
FOR THEY WILL SEE GOD.

He wants you to be pure in your motives, your life, your heart, your attitudes, the way you talk, the way you act, the jokes you tell—to be pure through and through. The way you look at people of the opposite sex should be pure so you are ready for the romantic relationship that God will have for you when it is the right time. You need to be committed to courtship and purity, not just pursuing any old dating relationship.

Take these two Scriptures today and practice self-control and purity of heart in all things. You will be a WorldChanger.

Humility and Hard Work

W e talked about *humility*.

1 PETER 5:6
HUMBLE YOURSELVES, THEREFORE, UNDER GOD'S MIGHTY HAND, THAT HE MAY
LIFT YOU UP IN DUE TIME.

Being humble is an incredible asset for a Christian. Being humble doesn't mean you are not strong. God wants you to be humble so you can honor your parents and so you can relate to other people. Remember, Moses was the meekest man on the earth. He was humble, but that doesn't mean he was weak. Moses had controlled power. Remember that you have to live a humble life. That doesn't mean that you let others run all over you. But you know who you are and you know who God is and you live with that in mind.

We also talked about being a *hard worker* and about the results of having this character trait in your life. The Bible talks about working with all of your heart as for the Lord.

COLOSSIANS 3:22-23
SLAVES, OBEY YOUR EARTHLY MASTERS IN EVERYTHING; AND DO IT, NOT ONLY
WHEN THEIR EYE IS ON YOU AND TO WIN THEIR FAVOR, BUT WITH SINCERITY OF
HEART AND REVERENCE FOR THE LORD. WHATEVER YOU DO, WORK AT IT WITH
ALL YOUR HEART, AS WORKING FOR THE LORD, NOT FOR MEN.

I want you to reaffirm your commitment to build the character trait of hard work into your life. Pour your guts into whatever you do. Don't be afraid to sweat. Especially when it comes to working with your church or your youth group, going on a mission trip, or doing something for God, make sure you always give your best and commit to work harder at it than you do anything else.

Take these two Scriptures with you all day today. Use them to renew your mind to develop a humble attitude. And show the world that you are not afraid to work hard for the kingdom of God.

Vision and Endurance

God wants you to be full of *vision*. A WorldChanger has to dare to dream. You must think big. A WorldChanger is full of faith and sees no obstacles.

> HEBREWS 11:1
> NOW FAITH IS BEING SURE OF WHAT WE HOPE FOR AND CERTAIN OF WHAT WE DO NOT SEE.

If you are full of vision, you can see the forest and not just the trees. You can see God's heart for the whole world and for the people around you.

We also talked about having *endurance*.

> MATTHEW 24:13
> HE WHO STANDS FIRM TO THE END WILL BE SAVED.

God is looking for people who will persevere and endure. It's going to take a lot of endurance to reach your city for God. It's going to take a lot of endurance to reach the world. God is looking for men and women who will take that endurance seriously and not play around with their walk with God. He is looking for people who are not going to fall for every little temptation. He wants people who are not going to fall every time there is a little pressure but who will endure and keep pushing and pushing until the end.

I want you to take these two Scriptures today and meditate on them. Use them to build vision, faith, and endurance into your life. Determine to be somebody who is full of faith and passion for God and who is committed to endure until the very end.

MISSIONS IS...
being able to see
God's hand move.
—Andrew

Living a New Standard

So, you've come to the end of this book, to the end of this devotional, but definitely not to the end of your character. This is only the beginning of living character every day. It's important to continue to develop your character. Work on a regular basis on the different areas of character that we have studied over the last several weeks. Earlier we talked about having a vision for your life in areas that you wanted to develop. I hope there were areas of character that you could see that you need to continue to develop and as a result have committed to keep working on these areas.

I want to give you something practical to do. Pick one character trait for each day or maybe for each week. Drill that thing into your life the same way we've done in this book. Just take one character trait at a time—whether it's having a passion for God, living with integrity, or having a pure heart—and concentrate on that one trait. Find other Scriptures that talk about that trait. Do research, ask other people, read books about it, and drill it into your life all day long so you are concentrating on building that trait into your life.

I want to encourage you to reaffirm your commitment to carry out the ten challenges of a WorldChanger. Don't just commit to living them for a week or a month, but endure to the end. As you assimilate these marks, these character traits, of a World-Changer into your life, you will have the resources to stand up and live all of the challenges. If you have not yet been on a mission trip, now is the time to sign up. Now is the time to GO.

As you continue to build your life on solid Christian character, you become a part of this army of tens of thousands of young people who are tired of being flaky Christians. They are tired of watching people get blown over. They are tired of getting blown over themselves. They are ready to stand up and be counted. They are ready to live a new standard that other people can look to and say, "That's what it's like to be a Christian." People will recognize that you have character. They'll see that you are committed to changing the world. They'll know that you do things that are noticeable to the people around you for the sake of the kingdom of God. You are not just yelling and screaming, but you are living a life of character in private and in public. They will see that you have become a part of making history while you are young. You have become a WorldChanger!

WorldChangers 2000

"Love the Lord your God with all your heart and with all your soul and with all your mind and with all your strength. . . . Love your neighbor as yourself."
—Mark 12:30–31

WorldChangers are people who take this Scripture seriously and who live it out every day of their lives.

With All Your Heart
- ☐ WorldChangers Keep Their Relationship with Jesus Alive by Keeping Their Quiet Times
- ☐ WorldChangers Systematically Study the Bible
- ☐ WorldChangers Are Committed to Their Church and Their Youth Group

With All Your Soul and with All Your Mind
- ☐ WorldChangers Commit Their Mind to God
- ☐ WorldChangers Pursue Holy Courtship Instead of Dating
- ☐ WorldChangers Honor Their Parents

With All Your Strength
- ☐ WorldChangers Have an Accountability Friendship
- ☐ WorldChangers Have a Lifestyle of Worship and Holy Actions
- ☐ WorldChangers Start a Revolution

Love Your Neighbor as Yourself
- ☐ WorldChangers Go on a Mission Trip While They're Teens

I commit to keep all 10 challenges throughout my teen years.

_____   _____

WorldChanger's Signature   *Date*

GET A SERIOUS CASE OF
HEARTBURN

An explosive video wall . . . live bands . . . hilarious skits . . . and blistering pyrotechnics make an Acquire the Fire™ weekend a total blast. But more than fun; this is for REAL! Acquire the Fire™ conventions are about getting tight with God . . . about making a radical commitment to Jesus Christ . . . about having a serious case of heartburn for God.

Acquire the Fire™ conventions are held in 27 cities across North America each year, reaching over 100,000 teens. Call us today to find out when Acquire the Fire™ will be in your region.
Don't miss out!
This is for you and your friends!

1-800-329-FIRE

ACQUIRE THE FIRE™
CONVENTIONS

SUMMER MISSIONS

"WORLDCHANGER"

FAST APPLICATION

Are you SERIOUS about wanting to make a commitment to take Christ to another nation next summer? Your first step is to fill out the application below and send it in. Be sure to fill out both sides.

Full Name (as written on birth certificate)

_____

LAST   FIRST   MIDDLE INITIAL

Social Security Number _____

Sex ❑M ❑F   Citizen of what nation? _____

Birth Date ___/___/___ Age _____ Height _____ Weight _____

Permanent Address

Street _____

City _____ State/Province _____ ZIP _____

Phone (_____) _____ Daytime Phone (_____) _____

Current Mailing Address (if different)

Street _____

City _____ State/Province _____ ZIP _____

Phone (_____) _____ Daytime Phone (_____) _____

How long at this address and number? _____

Guardian's Name _____

Guardian's Phone (_____) _____

List any Teen Mania missions trips you have taken:

      nation _____ date _____

      nation _____ date _____

      nation _____ date _____

Church Name _____

Pastor's Name _____

Church Address _____

Church Phone (_____) _____

How long have you been involved in this church? _____years

If you are in a dating relationship with someone, is this person
      applying to come on this trip? ❑Yes ❑No

If yes, what is this person's name? _____

● Have you ever been involved with (if so, please give the date of last involvement & explanation - use additional paper if necessary)
- ❑ alcohol
- ❑ illegal drugs
- ❑ a cult or the occult

● Have you ever (if so, please give date of last incident & explanation - use additional paper if necessary)
- ❑ been expelled from school?
- ❑ been placed in a juvenile detention center?
- ❑ been in jail?
- ❑ been under psychiatric care?
- ❑ had an eating disorder?
- ❑ had respiratory problems, seizures or fainting spells?
- ❑ had diabetes?

● Rank in order of importance (1 being the most important), any source(s) which have influenced you to come on this trip.
Give names where applicable:

____Ron Luce	____Acquire the Fire
____Magazine	____Maniac Friend
____Christian Musician	____Radio/TV Program
____TMM Intern(s)	____Recruiting Team
____This WorldChanger Book	____Other

❑ I am interested in a leadership position. Please send me an application. (Mission Advisors must be 18 & Team Leaders must be 21 years old)

SEND WITH YOUR APPLICATION

With your application, please include the following and you will be on your way to a WorldChanging summer.

- ❑ Two recent close-up nonreturnable photos of yourself (No group shots)
- ❑ $39.00 non-refundable application fee
- ❑ Parent's signature (if you're under 18)

We'll send you an additional packet
to complete your application process.

Send your application to:

TEEN MANIA MINISTRIES
P.O. Box 2000 • Garden Valley, TX 75790-2000
PHONE 1-800-299-TEEN

TAKE THEM TO OUR LEADER

What are the chances of having an unbelievably great, earth-shattering summer at home this year?

It could happen. If they decide to hold the Summer Olympics in your back yard. Fact is, the possibilities look pretty remote.

So maybe it's time to consider some other options. Like the tropical jungles of Panama. The snow-capped volcanoes of Ecuador. Or the great Kalahari Desert of Botswana.

The possibilities are endless . . . when you make your summer a Teen Mania summer. You'll see incredible sights. Experience exotic new cultures. But most importantly, you'll see people come to know Jesus. Teen Mania summer mission trips are designed around one goal: to bring the Gospel of our Lord to the unreached. The adventures, friendships, personal growth, and amazing memories simply come along for the ride.

We want you to join about 3,000 other teens from across North America who are going to tell the people in 20 nations about Jesus next summer. Not everyone knows who He is or why He came or what He wants to do in their lives. And that's where you come in. You go tell them!

Take the challenge. From past experience, we know that a lot of these people are going to respond to the gospel message - like about 100,000 people last year alone. Lives will be changed . . . forever, And you will be the one who helped make it happen. You will get to take them to our leader!

Don't miss out. This is what "changing the world" is all about.

FILL OUT THE
WORLDCHANGER APPLICATION
IN THIS BOOK OR
CALL 1-800-299-TEEN

Think of it as Clearasil® for your soul.

Worship For World Changers - the music of Teen Mania 1996.
Featuring thirteen awesome praise & worship songs,
a room full of "maniacs"
and special guests Anointed and Code Of Ethics.

Available at Christian bookstores everywhere.